Quick & Easy
Risotto and Rice

Contents

Introduction

Rice is the staple food for one-third of the world's population, its myriad varieties and sub-varieties appear in the cooking of all continents and so in countries as diverse as China and Italy, the Lebanon and Mexico. It is an ideal food for a host of reasons: it is easy to store and quick to cook, nutritious and easy to digest, extraordinarily versatile - and delicious.

Main Rice Varieties

Long-grain white rice is milled or polished to remove the outer husk, the germ, and most of the bran. The grain is long and opaque. Long-grain rice is sometimes called Patna rice, because it originated in Patna, India. It is a popular all-purpose rice, suitable for soups, stews, salads and pilafs. Long-grain rice should be light and fluffy when cooked, the grains separated.

Easy-cook rice is parboiled long-grain white rice. Rice was first parboiled in India to increase its shelf-life and hardness. Parboiling before milling forces the vitamins deeper into the grain, increasing its nutritional value. Parboiled rice is a golden colour.

Long-grain brown rice is milled to remove just the inedible husk, so it is less refined and a soft brown colour. It has a nutty flavour and a chewier texture than polished rice. It can be used instead of white rice in most recipes and is especially good in salads.

Basmati rice is sometimes called the champagne or king of rice. It is a long- and slim-grain rice grown in India and Pakistan, very white with a distinctive aroma essential to pilafs and biryanis. It is light and fluffy when cooked. Brown Basmati - milled to remove the husk only - is more nutritious, dense, and chewy than polished rice and takes longer to cook, 45–50 minutes. Storage time is limited, because its oils become rancid.

Italian risotto rice is a medium short-grain rice grown in northern Italy and used almost exclusively for risottos. It has a chalky line down the centre. The higher the quality, the more liquid it absorbs as it cooks. The superior varieties - arborio, carnaroli, roma, and vialone nano can absorb three to four times their volume. The cooked grains are separate and firm to the bite.

Spanish calaspara and **la bomba rice**, grown near Murcia and Valencia, are quality medium-short-grain rices especially for paella. Italian risotto rice may be used instead.

Pudding rice or **short-grain**, sometimes called Carolina rice, is a short- or round-grain chalky rice with a bland flavour. The cooked grains are moist and sticky, so ideal for puddings, custards, and croquettes of milk.

Thai fragrant rice or **jasmine rice** is a savoury white long-grain rice used in Thai and South East Asian cooking. It has a natural aromatic flavour and is slightly soft and sticky when cooked.

Japanese sushi or **sticky rice** is a short-grain, absorbent rice, perfect when grains must hold together in a shape for sushi. The opaque, pearl-like grains are white and round or slightly elongated. Sushi rice cooks in about 15–20 minutes by the absorption method; it is usually mixed with a seasoning of rice vinegar and sugar, then fanned to cool it and give it a shine.

Black sweet rice or black **glutinous rice** is an Asian medium short-grain rice with a dark purple-red colour. Its rich flavour stands up to very sweet ingredients such as coconut milk and palm sugar. It cooks in 25–30 minutes by the absorption method. The colour will dye other ingredients and cookware.

Camargue red rice from the South of France has a medium oval grain with a reddish brown colour. It has an earthy taste and a firm, chewy texture. Although it loses colour in cooking, it looks appetizing and stands up to robust flavours. It needs a cooking time of 45–60 minutes by simmering or the absorption method.

Wild rice is not a true rice, but an aquatic grass. It has a delicious, nutty flavour. The long, glossy brown-black grains 'flower' as they cook. Wild rice is expensive, so is often packaged with long-grain rices.

Other Rice Products

Ground rice and rice flour are made by milling white rice to a flourlike consistency varying in coarseness from slightly granular for ground rice to very fine for rice flour.

Rice Flakes are usually used for thickening in the Far East. They may be deep-fried and used as a garnish

Rice Noodles, vermicelli and rice sticks, are dry, rice flour-based pasta, twisted into skeins. They range in size from very fine (sen mee), to about 3 mm/⅛ inch thick - like tagliatelle (sen lek) - to about 1 cm/½ inch wide (sen yaai). Rehydrate in hot water for 5–20 minutes and drain.

Japanese harusame noodles are very thin noodles; treat as rice vermicelli.

Vietnamese rice paper wrappers are used for spring rolls and 'wraps'. Moisten by dipping briefly into water or spraying, and eat, or steam, or fry them.

Rice paper is an edible paper, thin and very brittle, made from ricelike plants.

Rice vinegars are wine-based and may be clear, yellow, red or black and mellow in flavour to rich and fruity. Japanese saké is a rice wine with a distinctive flavour, and mirin is sweetened rice wine.

Cooking Methods

The cooking method depends on the type of rice, so you must choose the correct rice for your recipe. As a rough guide, allow 2 tablespoons of raw brown rice per serving, and 55 g/2 oz for other varieties; pudding recipes vary. Choose one of the following cooking methods:

Simmering is easy, but gives least flavour. Boil a pan of water, add a pinch of salt, sprinkle in the rice, and return to the boil. Reduce the heat to medium.

The Absorption Method uses exactly as much liquid as the rice will absorb. Put the rice in a heavy-based pan, add a pinch of salt, a tablespoon of oil (optional) and 1½ times the amount of cold water. Bring to the boil over a high heat, then reduce the heat to very low and simmer, tightly covered, for the times given above until all the liquid is absorbed. Uncovering the pan lets the steam escape, altering the measured amount of liquid; stirring can break the fragile rice grains, releasing sticky starch.

Remove the pan from the heat and stand for 5 minutes, then fluff with a fork into a warm serving bowl. Alternatively, remove from the heat, uncover, and place a tea towel or folded kitchen paper over the rice, re-cover, and stand for 5 minutes. This absorbs the steam, preventing it from dripping back into the rice.

The Pilaf Method In a heavy-based saucepan over medium heat, warm two tablespoons of oil or butter and cook a finely chopped onion or 2–3 shallots. Add the rice and cook, stirring frequently, until it is well coated with fat and translucent. Add 1½ times stock or water, a pinch of salt, and bring to the boil, stirring once or twice. Now cover the surface with a round of non-stick baking paper (to reduce the speed of evaporation) and cover tightly. Reduce the heat as low as possible.

Cooking Times

White basmati rice: 10–12 minutes.
Long-grain white rice: 15–18 minutes
Easy-cook: 20–25 minutes
Brown rice: 35–40 minutes
Wild rice: 55-60 minutes

KEY

Simplicity level 1-3 (1 easiest, 3 slightly harder)
Preparation time
Cooking time

Broccoli Soup with Cream

This soup highlights the rich flavour of healthy green broccoli. To make a smooth soup, purée the cooked ingredients before serving.

NUTRITIONAL INFORMATION

Calories	395	Sugars	5g
Protein	7g	Fat	35g
Carbohydrate	13g	Saturates	21g

5 mins

45–50 mins

SERVES 4

INGREDIENTS

- 400 g/14 oz broccoli (from 1 large head)
- 2 tsp butter
- 1 tsp oil
- 1 onion, chopped finely
- 1 leek, thinly sliced
- 1 small carrot, chopped finely
- 3 tbsp white rice
- 850 ml/1½ pints water
- 1 bay leaf
- freshly grated nutmeg
- 4 tbsp double cream
- 100 g/3½ oz soft cheese
- salt and pepper
- croûtons, to serve (see Cook's Tip)

1 Divide the broccoli into small florets and cut off the stems. Peel the large stems. Chop all the stems into small pieces.

2 Heat the butter and oil in a large saucepan over a medium heat and add the onion, leek and carrot. Cook for 3–4 minutes, stirring frequently, until the onion is soft.

3 Add the broccoli stems, rice, water, bay leaf and a pinch of salt. Bring just to the boil and reduce the heat to low. Cover and simmer for 15 minutes. Add the florets and continue cooking, covered, for 15–20 minutes until the rice and the vegetables are tender. Remove the bay leaf.

4 Season the soup with grated nutmeg, black pepper and, if needed, more salt. Stir in the double cream and soft cheese. Simmer over a low heat for a few minutes until heated through, stirring occasionally. Taste, and adjust the seasoning as required. Ladle into warm soup bowls and serve sprinkled with croûtons.

COOK'S TIP

To make croûtons, remove the crusts from thick slices of bread, then dice the bread. Fry it in vegetable oil, stirring constantly, until evenly browned, then drain on kitchen paper.

Saffron Fish Soup

This soup makes a good starter for a dinner party. The saffron-flavoured base may be prepared in advance and the fish cooked at the last moment.

NUTRITIONAL INFORMATION

Calories	329	Sugars	8g
Protein	19g	Fat	18g
Carbohydrate	17g	Saturates	11g

5 mins 40 mins

SERVES 4

INGREDIENTS

- 2 tsp butter
- 1 onion, chopped finely
- 1 leek, thinly sliced
- 1 carrot, sliced thinly
- pinch of saffron threads
- 4 tbsp white rice
- 125 ml/4 fl oz dry white wine
- 1 litre/1¾ pints fish stock
- 125 ml/4 fl oz double cream
- 350 g/12 oz skinless white fish fillet, such as cod, haddock or monkfish, cut into 1 cm/½ inch cubes
- 4 tomatoes, skinned, deseeded and chopped
- 3 tbsp snipped fresh chives
- salt and pepper

1 Heat the butter in a saucepan over a medium heat and add the onion, leek and carrot. Cook for 3–4 minutes, stirring frequently, until the onion is soft.

2 Add the saffron, rice, wine and stock. Bring just to the boil, then reduce the heat to low. Season with salt and pepper. Cover and simmer for 20 minutes, or until the rice and vegetables are soft.

3 Let the soup cool slightly, then transfer it to a blender or a food processor and purée until smooth, working in batches if necessary. (If using a food processor, strain off the cooking liquid and reserve. Purée the soup solids with enough cooking liquid to moisten them, then combine with the remaining liquid.)

4 Return the soup to the saucepan, stir in the cream and simmer over a low heat for a few minutes until heated through, stirring occasionally.

5 Season the fish and add, with the chopped tomatoes, to the simmering soup. Cook for 3–5 minutes, or until the fish is just tender.

6 Stir in most of the chives. Taste the soup and adjust the seasoning, if necessary. Ladle into warm shallow soup bowls, sprinkle the remaining fresh chives on top, and serve.

Garlic Fish Soup

The delicate colour of this soup belies its heady flavours. The recipe has been adapted from a French soup thickened with a garlicky mayonnaise.

NUTRITIONAL INFORMATION

Calories	191	Sugars	4g
Protein	19g	Fat	7g
Carbohydrate	12g	Saturates	3g

5 mins — 40–45 mins

SERVES 4–5

INGREDIENTS

- 2 tsp olive oil
- 1 large onion, chopped
- 1 small fennel bulb, chopped
- 1 leek, sliced
- 3–4 large garlic cloves, thinly sliced
- 125 ml/4 fl oz dry white wine
- 1.2 litres/2 pints fish stock
- 4 tbsp white rice
- 1 strip pared lemon rind
- 1 bay leaf
- 450 g/1 lb skinless white fish fillets, cut into 4 cm/1½ inch pieces
- 50 ml/2 fl oz double cream
- 2 tbsp chopped fresh parsley
- salt and pepper

1 Heat the oil in a large saucepan over a medium-low heat. Add the onion, fennel, leek and garlic and then cook for 4–5 minutes, stirring frequently, until the onion is softened.

2 Add the wine and bubble briefly. Add the fish stock, rice, lemon rind and bay leaf. Bring the mixture to the boil, reduce the heat to medium-low and simmer for 20–25 minutes, or until the rice and vegetables are soft. Remove the lemon rind and bay leaf from the pan.

3 Let the soup cool slightly, then transfer to a blender or a food processor and purée until smooth, working in batches if necessary. (If using a food processor, strain off the cooking liquid and reserve. Purée the soup solids with enough cooking liquid to moisten them, then combine with the remaining liquid.)

4 Return the puréed soup to the saucepan and bring to a simmer. Add the fish pieces to the soup, cover, and continue simmering on a low heat, stirring occasionally, for 4–5 minutes, or until the fish is cooked and begins to flake. Stir in the cream. Taste and adjust the seasoning, adding salt, if needed, and pepper. Ladle into warm soup bowls and serve sprinkled with parsley.

Turkey & Sage Soup

This is a warming soup for winter, substantial enough to present as a one-dish lunch or supper, served with plenty of crusty bread.

NUTRITIONAL INFORMATION

Calories	470	Sugars	4g
Protein	18g	Fat	30g
Carbohydrate	34g	Saturates	18g

5 mins — 50 mins

SERVES 4–5

INGREDIENTS

- 3 tbsp butter
- 1 onion, chopped finely
- 1 celery stick, chopped finely
- 25 large fresh sage leaves, chopped finely
- 4 tbsp plain flour
- 1.2 litres/2 pints turkey or chicken stock
- 100 g/3½ oz brown rice
- 250 g/9 oz mushrooms, sliced
- 200 g/7 oz cooked turkey
- 200 ml/7 fl oz double cream
- salt and pepper
- freshly grated Parmesan cheese, to serve

1 Melt half the butter in a large saucepan over a medium-low heat. Add the onion, celery and sage and cook for 3–4 minutes until the onion is softened, stirring frequently. Stir in the flour and continue cooking for 2 minutes.

2 Slowly add a quarter of the stock and stir well, scraping the bottom of the pan to mix in the flour. Stir in the rest of the stock and bring just to the boil.

3 Stir in the rice, and season to taste. Reduce the heat and simmer gently, partially covered, for about 30 minutes, or until the rice is tender, stirring occasionally.

4 Meanwhile, melt the remaining butter in a large frying pan over a medium heat. Add the mushrooms and season with salt and pepper. Cook for about 8 minutes until the mushrooms are golden brown, stirring occasionally at first, then more often after they start to colour. Add the mushrooms to the soup.

5 Add the turkey to the soup and stir in the cream. Continue simmering for about 10 minutes until heated through. Taste and adjust the seasoning, if necessary. Ladle into warm soup bowls and serve with Parmesan cheese.

Rice Soup with Eggs

This classic Eastern soup is sometimes eaten for breakfast in Thailand. This version is a tasty way of using up leftover cooked rice.

NUTRITIONAL INFORMATION

Calories	197	Sugars	1g
Protein	11g	Fat	10g
Carbohydrate	17g	Saturates	2g

5 mins | 10–15 mins

SERVES 4

INGREDIENTS

- 1 tsp sunflower oil
- 1 garlic clove, crushed
- 50 g/1¾ oz minced pork
- 3 spring onions, sliced
- 1 tbsp grated fresh root ginger
- 1 red bird-eye chilli, deseeded and chopped
- 1 litre/1¾ pints chicken stock
- 200 g/7 oz cooked long-grain rice
- 1 tbsp Thai fish sauce
- 4 small eggs
- salt and pepper
- 2 tbsp shredded fresh coriander, to garnish

1 Heat the oil in a large pan or wok. Add the garlic and pork and fry gently for about 1 minute, or until the meat is broken up but not browned.

2 Stir in the spring onions, grated root ginger, bird-eye chilli and chicken stock, and bring the mixture to a boil, stirring. Add the cooked rice, lower the heat and simmer for 2 minutes.

3 Add the fish sauce and adjust the seasoning with salt and pepper to taste. Carefully break the eggs into the soup and simmer over a very low heat for 3–4 minutes, or until set.

4 Ladle the rice soup into large individual bowls, allowing 1 egg per portion. Garnish each portion with shredded fresh coriander and serve.

COOK'S TIP

Beat the eggs together and fry the mixture like an omelette until it is set, then cut into strips and add them to the soup just before serving.

Dolmas

These stuffed vine leaves are a Greek-style starter. You will need a large frying pan with a lid to hold all the stuffed vine leaves in a single layer.

NUTRITIONAL INFORMATION

Calories	82	Sugars	2g
Protein	1g	Fat	7g
Carbohydrate	5g	Saturates	1g

15–20 mins   40–45 mins

MAKES 25–30

INGREDIENTS

- 225 g/8 oz package vine leaves preserved in brine, about 40 leaves in total
- 150 ml/5 fl oz olive oil
- 4 tbsp lemon juice
- 300 ml/10 fl oz water
- lemon wedges, to serve

STUFFING

- 125 g/4½ oz long-grain rice, not basmati
- 350 ml/12 fl oz water
- 55 g/2 oz currants
- 55 g/2 oz pine kernels, chopped
- 2 spring onions, chopped very finely
- 4 tbsp very finely chopped fresh parsley
- 1 tbsp very finely chopped fresh mint
- 1 tbsp very finely chopped fresh coriander
- 1 tbsp very finely chopped fresh dill
- finely grated rind of ½ lemon
- salt and pepper

1 Rinse the vine leaves and place them in a heatproof bowl. Pour over enough boiling water to cover and leave to soak for 5 minutes. Drain well.

2 Meanwhile, place the rice and water in a pan with a pinch of salt and bring to the boil. Lower the heat, cover and simmer for 10–12 minutes, or until all the liquid is absorbed. Drain and set aside to cool.

3 Stir the currants, pine kernels, spring onions, fresh herbs and grated lemon rind into the cooled rice. Season well with salt and pepper.

4 Line the bottom of a large frying pan with 3 or 4 of the thickest vine leaves, or any that are torn.

5 Put a vine leaf on the work surface, vein-side upwards, with the pointed end facing away from you. Put a small, compact roll of the stuffing at the base of the leaf. Fold up the bottom end of the leaf.

6 Fold in each side to overlap in the centre. Roll up the leaf around the filling. Squeeze lightly in your hand. Continue with the remaining leaves.

7 Place the leaf rolls in a single layer in the pan, seam-side down. Combine the olive oil, lemon juice and water, then pour into the pan.

8 Fit a heatproof plate over the rolls and cover the pan. Simmer for 30 minutes. Remove from the heat and let the stuffed vine leaves cool in the liquid. Serve chilled with lemon wedges.

5

6

Lemon Risotto

This is a stylish first course, with a delicate aroma and a fresh taste that together stimulate the taste buds for the main course to follow.

NUTRITIONAL INFORMATION

Calories	442	Sugars	3g
Protein	6g	Fat	15g
Carbohydrate	68g	Saturates	6g

10 mins — 30 mins

SERVES 4

INGREDIENTS

- 2–3 lemons
- 2 tbsp olive oil
- 2 shallots, chopped finely
- 300 g/10½ oz risotto rice
- 125 ml/4 fl oz dry white vermouth
- 1 litre/1¾ pints vegetable or chicken stock, simmering
- 1 tbsp very, very finely chopped fresh flat-leaved parsley
- 2 tbsp butter
- freshly pared Parmesan cheese, to serve
- avocado slices, to serve

TO GARNISH

- thin strips of pared lemon rind
- fresh parsley sprigs

2

4

5

1 Finely grate the rind from 2 lemons. Firmly roll the rindless lemons backwards and forwards on a board, then squeeze 100 ml/3½ fl oz juice. If you don't have enough, squeeze another lemon. Set the rind and juice aside.

2 Heat the olive oil in a heavy-based saucepan. Add the chopped shallots and fry, stirring, for about 3 minutes until soft. Add the rice and stir until all the grains are well coated.

3 Stir in the vermouth and bubble until it evaporates. Lower the heat to medium-low. Add the lemon juice and a ladleful of simmering stock. Stir together, then let simmer, only stirring occasionally, until all the liquid is absorbed.

4 Add another ladleful of stock and stir, then let simmer until absorbed. Continue adding stock in this way, letting it be absorbed by the rice after each addition, until all of the stock has been used up and the risotto is creamy, with several tablespoons of liquid floating on the surface.

5 Stir in the lemon rind and parsley. Add the butter, then cover and remove from the heat. Let stand for 5 minutes. Stir well and then garnish with strips of lemon rind and parsley. Serve with Parmesan cheese and avocado slices.

Fragrant Asparagus Risotto

Soft, creamy rice combines with the flavours of citrus and light aniseed to make this a delicious supper for four or a substantial starter for six.

NUTRITIONAL INFORMATION

Calories	223	Sugars	9g
Protein	6g	Fat	6g
Carbohydrate	40g	Saturates	1g

10 mins 45 mins

SERVES 4

INGREDIENTS

- 115 g/4 oz fine asparagus spears, trimmed
- 1.2 litres/2 pints vegetable stock
- 2 bulbs fennel
- 2 tbsp low-fat spread
- 1 tsp olive oil
- 2 celery sticks, trimmed and chopped
- 2 medium leeks, trimmed and shredded
- 350 g/12 oz arborio rice
- 3 medium oranges
- salt and pepper

1 Bring a small pan of water to the boil and cook the asparagus for 1 minute. Drain and set aside until required.

2 Pour the stock into a saucepan and bring to the boil. Reduce the heat to maintain a gentle simmer.

3 Meanwhile, trim the fennel, reserving the fronds. Use a sharp knife to cut the fennel into thin slices.

4 Carefully melt the low-fat spread with the oil in a large saucepan, taking care that the water in the low-fat spread does not evaporate. Gently fry the fennel, celery and leeks for 3–4 minutes, or until just softened. Add the rice and cook, stirring, for another 2 minutes until mixed.

5 Add a ladleful of stock to the pan and cook gently, stirring, until the liquid is absorbed by the rice.

6 Continue stirring in the stock, about half a ladleful at a time, letting each addition be absorbed by the rice before adding the next. This should take about 20–25 minutes. The finished risotto should have a creamy consistency and the rice should be tender, but firm to the bite.

7 Finely grate the rind of 1 orange and extract the juice, and mix both in to the rice. Carefully remove the peel and pith from the remaining oranges. Holding the fruit over the saucepan, cut out the orange segments and add to the rice, along with any juice that falls.

8 Stir in the orange, then stir in the asparagus spears. Season the risotto to taste and garnish with the fennel fronds.

4

5

7

Risi e Bisi

This famous Venetian rice soup makes a very substantial first course - or a one-dish meal. It should be thick but not as thick as a risotto.

NUTRITIONAL INFORMATION

Calories	464	Sugars	10g
Protein	19g	Fat	20g
Carbohydrate	56g	Saturates	12g

10 mins — 35 mins

SERVES 4

INGREDIENTS

- 900 g/2 lb fresh unshelled peas
- 4 tbsp unsalted butter
- 1 onion, chopped finely
- 850 ml/1½ pints chicken stock
- 200 g/7 oz arborio rice
- 2 tbsp chopped fresh flat-leaved parsley
- 55 g/2 oz freshly grated Parmesan cheese
- salt and pepper

TO GARNISH

- tomato slices
- Parmesan cheese shavings
- fresh basil leaves

1 Remove the fresh peas from their shells. The shelled peas should weigh about 300 g/10½ oz.

2 Melt the butter in a large heavy-based saucepan over a medium heat. Add the chopped onion and cook for about 2 minutes, stirring occasionally, until beginning to soften.

3 Add the shelled peas and cook, stirring occasionally, for a further 2–3 minutes. Gradually add the chicken stock and bring the mixture to the boil. Reduce the heat and simmer, covered, for about 10 minutes, stirring occasionally.

4 Add the rice and season with a little salt and pepper. Simmer, covered, for about 15 minutes, stirring occasionally, until the rice is just tender.

5 Stir in the parsley and adjust the seasoning. If the soup is too thick, add a little more stock. Stir in the Parmesan, then ladle into bowls.

6 Serve garnished with tomato slices, Parmesan shavings and basil leaves.

2

3

5

COOK'S TIP

You can substitute 300 g/10½ oz frozen peas for fresh: defrost under running hot water, add to the softened onions and cook for about 5 minutes with the stock. Continue from step 4.

Tomato & Red Rice Soup

Red rice, with its firm texture and nutty flavour, is an unusual addition to this soup, but long-grain brown rice can be used instead.

NUTRITIONAL INFORMATION

Calories	150	Sugars	8g
Protein	3g	Fat	5g
Carbohydrate	24g	Saturates	1g

5 mins

55 mins

SERVES 4–6

INGREDIENTS

- 2 tbsp olive oil
- 1 onion, chopped finely
- 1 carrot, chopped finely
- 1 celery stick, chopped finely
- 3–4 garlic cloves, chopped finely
- 900 g/2 lb fresh ripe tomatoes, skinned, deseeded and chopped finely (see Cook's Tip)
- 1 bay leaf
- ½ cinnamon stick (optional)
- 1 tsp fresh thyme leaves or ½ tsp dried thyme
- 1 tsp dried oregano
- 1 tbsp brown sugar
- ½ tsp cayenne pepper, or to taste
- 1.5 litres/2¾ pints chicken stock or water
- 100 g/3½ oz red rice or long-grain brown rice
- 1 tbsp chopped oregano leaves, to garnish
- salt and pepper
- freshly grated Parmesan cheese, to serve

1 Heat the oil in a large saucepan over a medium heat. Add the onion, carrot and celery and cook for about 10 minutes, stirring occasionally, until soft. Stir in the garlic and cook for another minute.

2 Add the tomatoes, bay leaf, cinnamon stick (if using), thyme, dried oregano, sugar and cayenne pepper, then cook, stirring occasionally, for about 5 minutes, or until the tomatoes begin to cook down.

3 Add the stock and the rice and bring to the boil, skimming off any foam. Reduce the heat and simmer, covered, for about 30 minutes, or until the rice is tender, adding more stock if necessary.

4 Stir in the fresh oregano leaves and season with salt and pepper. Serve immediately, with grated Parmesan cheese for sprinkling.

1

2

4

COOKS' TIP

You need well-flavoured tomatoes for this soup; if they are unavailable, use canned Italian plum tomatoes and reduce the amount of stock if the tin contains a large amount of juice.

Vegetable Biryani

The Biryani originated in North India, where it became a traditional festival dish. The vegetables are flavoured with a yogurt-based marinade.

NUTRITIONAL INFORMATION

Calories	449	Sugars	18g
Protein	12g	Fat	12g
Carbohydrate	79g	Saturates	6g

2¼ hrs — 1 hr 5 mins

SERVES 4

INGREDIENTS

- 1 large potato, cubed
- 100 g/3½ oz baby carrots
- 50 g/1¾ oz okra, thickly sliced
- 2 celery sticks, sliced
- 75 g/2¾ oz baby button mushrooms, halved
- 1 aubergine, halved and sliced
- 300 ml/10 fl oz natural yogurt
- 1 tbsp grated fresh root ginger
- 2 large onions, grated
- 4 garlic cloves, crushed
- 1 tsp turmeric
- 1 tbsp curry powder
- 2 tbsp butter
- 2 onions, sliced
- 225 g/8 oz basmati rice
- chopped fresh coriander, to garnish

1 Cook the potato cubes, carrots and okra in a pan of boiling salted water for 7–8 minutes. Drain well and place in a large bowl. Mix with the celery, mushrooms and aubergine.

2 Mix the natural yogurt, grated fresh root ginger, grated onions, garlic, turmeric and curry powder and spoon over the vegetables. Set aside in a cool place to marinate for at least 2 hours.

3 Heat the butter in a heavy-based frying pan. Add the sliced onions and cook over a medium heat for 5–6 minutes, or until golden brown. Remove a few onions from the pan and reserve for the garnish.

4 Cook the rice in a large pan of boiling water for 7 minutes. Drain thoroughly and set aside.

5 Add the marinated vegetables to the onions and cook for 10 minutes.

6 Spoon half of the cooked rice into a 2 litre/3½ pint casserole dish. Spoon the vegetables over the top and cover with the remaining rice. Cover and cook in a preheated oven, 190°C/375°F/Gas Mark 5, for 20–25 minutes, or until the rice is tender.

7 Spoon the biryani on to a serving plate, garnish with the reserved onions and coriander, and serve.

2

3

6

Risotto Verde

An unusual combination of herbs and spinach mixed with arborio rice makes an attractive risotto on a colour theme of green.

NUTRITIONAL INFORMATION

Calories	374	Sugars	5g
Protein	10g	Fat	9g
Carbohydrate	55g	Saturates	2g

5 mins — 35 mins

SERVES 4

INGREDIENTS

- 1.7 litres/3 pints vegetable stock
- 2 tbsp olive oil
- 2 garlic cloves, crushed
- 2 leeks, shredded
- 225 g/8 oz arborio rice
- 300 ml/10 fl oz dry white wine
- 4 tbsp chopped mixed herbs
- 225 g/8 oz baby spinach
- 3 tbsp natural yogurt
- salt and pepper
- shredded leek, to garnish

1 Pour the stock into a large saucepan and bring to the boil. Reduce the heat to a simmer.

2 Meanwhile, heat the oil in a separate pan. Add the garlic and leeks and sauté over a low heat, stirring occasionally, for 2–3 minutes, until softened.

3 Stir in the rice and cook for 2 minutes, stirring to coat each grain with oil.

4 Pour in half of the wine and a little of the hot stock. Cook over a low heat until all of the liquid has been absorbed. Continue stirring in the stock and the wine, about half a ladleful at a time, letting each addition be absorbed before adding the next. This should take about 20–25 minutes. The risotto should be creamy and the rice tender, but firm to the bite.

5 Stir in the chopped mixed herbs and baby spinach, season to taste with salt and pepper and cook for 2 minutes.

6 Stir in the natural yogurt. Transfer to a warm serving dish, garnish with the shredded leek and serve immediately.

3

4

5

COOK'S TIP

Do not try to hurry the process of cooking the risotto as the rice must absorb the liquid slowly in order for it to reach the correct consistency.

Thai-spiced Sausages

These mildly spiced little sausages are a good choice for a buffet meal. They can be made a day in advance, and are equally good served hot or cold.

NUTRITIONAL INFORMATION

Calories	206	Sugars	0.1g
Protein	22g	Fat	11g
Carbohydrate	4g	Saturates	2g

5–10 mins 10–20 mins

SERVES 4

INGREDIENTS

- 400 g/14 oz lean minced pork
- 50 g/1¾ oz cooked rice
- 1 garlic clove, crushed
- 1 tsp Thai red curry paste
- 1 tsp ground black pepper
- 1 tsp ground coriander
- ½ tsp salt
- 3 tbsp lime juice
- 2 tbsp chopped fresh coriander
- 3 tbsp groundnut oil
- coconut sambal or soy sauce, to serve

1 Place the pork, rice, garlic, curry paste, pepper, ground coriander, salt, lime juice and chopped coriander in a bowl and knead together with your hands to mix.

1

2

3

2 Use your hands to shape the mixture into 12 small sausage shapes. If you can buy sausage casings, fill the casings with the mixture, then twist the filled casing at regular intervals to separate the mixture into small sausages, and cut where twisted to separate the sausages.

3 Heat the oil in a large frying pan over a medium heat. Add the sausages, in batches if necessary, and then fry for 8–10 minutes, turning them over occasionally to prevent burning, until they are a golden brown. Serve hot with a coconut sambal or soy sauce.

COOK'S TIP

These sausages can also be served as a starter – shape the mixture slightly smaller to make about 16 bite-sized sausages. Serve with a soy dip.

Stir-fried Rice with Egg

This is one of many Thai rice dishes made from leftover rice. Chilli flowers and spirals fashioned from egg rolls make this simple dish look attractive.

NUTRITIONAL INFORMATION

Calories	334	Sugars	49g
Protein	7g	Fat	9g
Carbohydrate	60g	Saturates	1g

5–10 mins   5 mins

SERVES 4

INGREDIENTS

2 tbsp groundnut oil

1 egg, beaten with 1 tsp water

1 garlic clove, chopped finely

1 small onion, chopped finely

1 tbsp Thai red curry paste

250 g/9 oz long-grain rice, cooked

55 g/2 oz cooked peas

1 tbsp Thai fish sauce

2 tbsp tomato ketchup

2 tbsp chopped fresh coriander

TO GARNISH

red chillies

cucumber slices

1 To make chilli flowers for the garnish, hold the stem of each chilli with your fingertips and use a small sharp, pointed knife to cut a slit down the length from near the stem end to the tip. Turn the chilli about a quarter turn and make another cut. Repeat to make a total of 4 cuts, then scrape out the seeds. Cut each 'petal' again in half, or into quarters, to make 8–16 petals. Place the chilli in iced water.

2 Heat about 1 teaspoon of the oil in a wok. Pour in the egg mixture, swirling it to coat the pan evenly and make a thin layer. When set and golden, remove the egg from the pan and roll up. Keep to one side.

3 Add the remaining oil to the pan and stir-fry the garlic and onion for 1 minute. Add the curry paste, then stir in the rice and peas.

4 Stir in the fish sauce and ketchup. Remove the pan from the heat and pile the rice on to a serving dish.

5 Slice the egg roll into spiral strips, without unrolling, and use to garnish the rice. Sprinkle with coriander, then add the cucumber slices and chilli flowers. Serve hot.

1

2

3

Smoked Chicken Chowder

Wild rice gives a wonderful texture to soups, and its nuttiness complements the rich flavour of smoked chicken.

NUTRITIONAL INFORMATION

Calories	322	Sugars	4g
Protein	14g	Fat	19g
Carbohydrate	25g	Saturates	9g

5 mins — 1–1¼ hrs

SERVES 6–8

INGREDIENTS

- 75 g/2¾ oz wild rice, washed
- 3 fresh corn-on-the-cobs, husks and silks removed
- 2 tbsp vegetable oil
- 1 large onion, chopped finely
- 1 celery stick, sliced thinly
- 1 leek, trimmed and sliced thily
- ½ tsp dried thyme
- 2 tbsp plain flour
- 1 litre/1¾ pints chicken stock
- 250 g/9 oz boned smoked chicken, skinned, diced or shredded
- 225 ml/8 fl oz double or whipping cream
- 1 tbsp chopped fresh dill
- salt and pepper
- fresh dill sprigs, to garnish

1 Bring a large saucepan of water to the boil. Add a tablespoon of salt and sprinkle in the wild rice. Return to the boil, then reduce the heat and simmer, covered, for about 40 minutes, or until just tender, but still firm to the bite. Do not overcook the rice as it will continue to cook in the soup. Drain and rinse, then set aside.

2 While the rice is cooking, prepare the vegetables. Hold the corn cobs vertical to a cutting board and, using a sharp heavy knife, cut down along the cobs to remove the kernels. Set aside the kernels. Scrape the cob to remove the milky juices; reserve the juices for the soup.

3 Heat the oil in a large pan over a medium heat. Add the onion, celery, leek and dried thyme. Cook, stirring frequently, for about 8 minutes, or until the vegetables are very soft.

4 Sprinkle over the flour and stir until blended. Gradually whisk in the stock, add the corn kernels with any juices, and bring to the boil. Skim off any foam. Reduce the heat and simmer for about 25 minutes, or until the vegetables are very soft and tender.

5 Stir in the smoked chicken, wild rice, cream and dill. Season to taste. Simmer for 10 minutes until the chicken and rice are heated through. Garnish with dill sprigs and serve immediately.

2

4

5

Tomato & Pecorino Risotto

Pecorino is an Italian cheese made from sheep's milk. Aged pecorino from Sardinia – *pecorino sardo* – is particularly good for this dish.

NUTRITIONAL INFORMATION

Calories	436	Sugars	8g
Protein	15g	Fat	14g
Carbohydrate	66g	Saturates	5g

40 mins 40 mins

SERVES 6

INGREDIENTS

- about 12 sun-dried tomatoes, not in oil
- 2 tbsp olive oil
- 1 large onion, chopped finely
- 4–6 garlic cloves, chopped finely
- 400 g/14 oz arborio or carnaroli rice
- 1.5 litres/2¾ pints chicken or vegetable stock, simmering
- 2 tbsp chopped fresh flat-leaved parsley
- 115 g/4 oz grated aged pecorino cheese
- extra virgin olive oil, for drizzling

1

5

6

1 Place the sun-dried tomatoes in a bowl and pour over enough boiling water to cover. Stand for about 30 minutes, or until soft and supple. Drain and pat dry, then shred thinly and set aside.

2 Heat the oil in a heavy-based pan over a medium heat. Add the onion and cook for about 2 minutes, until beginning to soften. Add the garlic and cook for 15 seconds. Add the rice and cook, stirring frequently, for 2 minutes, or until the rice is translucent and well coated with oil.

3 Add a ladleful of the hot stock, which will bubble and steam rapidly. Cook gently, stirring constantly, until the liquid has been absorbed.

4 Continue adding the stock, about half a ladleful at a time, letting each addition be absorbed by the rice before adding the next.

5 After about 15 minutes, stir in the sun-dried tomatoes. Continue to cook, adding the stock, until the rice is tender, but firm to the bite. The risotto should have a creamy consistency.

6 Remove from the heat and stir in the parsley and half the cheese. Cover, stand for about 1 minute, then spoon into serving dishes. Drizzle with extra virgin olive oil and sprinkle the remaining cheese over the top. Serve immediately.

Fideos Tostados

A staple of Spanish cooking, and eaten for centuries by Sephardic Jews from Spain, is the very thin, vermicelli-like pasta called *fideos*.

NUTRITIONAL INFORMATION

Calories	327	Sugars	3g
Protein	9g	Fat	7g
Carbohydrate	39g	Saturates	1g

5 mins   30–35 mins

SERVES 6

INGREDIENTS

- 350 g/12 oz vermicelli or angel hair pasta in coils, roughly broken
- 100 g/3½ oz long-grain white rice
- 3 tbsp extra virgin olive oil
- 200 g/7 oz canned chopped tomatoes, drained
- 600 ml/1 pint chicken stock or water, plus extra if necessary
- 1 bay leaf
- 1–2 tsp chopped fresh oregano or 1 tsp dried oregano
- ½ tsp dried thyme leaves
- salt and pepper
- 1–2 tbsp chopped fresh oregano or thyme, plus sprigs, to garnish

1 Put the pasta and rice in a dry, large, heavy-based saucepan or flameproof casserole over a medium-high heat and cook for 5–7 minutes, stirring frequently, until light golden. (The pasta will break unevenly, but this does not matter.)

2 Stir in 2 tablespoons of the olive oil, together with the chopped tomatoes, stock, bay leaf, oregano and thyme, then season with about a teaspoon of salt and pepper to taste.

3 Bring to the boil, reduce the heat to medium and simmer for 8 minutes, stirring frequently, to help unwind and separate the pasta coils.

4 Reduce the heat to low and cook, covered, for about 10 minutes, until the rice and pasta are tender and all the liquid absorbed. If the rice and pasta are too firm, add about 125 ml/4 fl oz more stock or water and continue to cook, covered, for a further 5 minutes. Remove from the heat.

5 Fluff up the rice and pasta with a fork while transferring it into a warmed serving bowl. Drizzle oil over the top, sprinkle with herbs, and serve immediately.

1

2

3

Red Rice Pilaf

Red rice from the Camargue region in the South of France has a robust, aromatic, nutty flavour which complements roasted vegetables.

NUTRITIONAL INFORMATION

Calories	773	Sugars	30g
Protein	11g	Fat	42g
Carbohydrate	94g	Saturates	9g

5–10 mins 55 mins

SERVES 4–6

INGREDIENTS

- 125 ml/4 fl oz olive oil
- grated rind and juice of 1 orange
- 2 tbsp balsamic vinegar
- 2 tsp coriander seeds, lightly crushed
- 1 bay leaf
- ½ tsp crushed dried chillies, or to taste
- 8–10 small raw beetroots, trimmed, scrubbed and halved
- 250 g/9 oz shallots or baby onions
- 6–8 baby parsnips, trimmed
- 4–6 baby carrots, trimmed
- 1 tsp chopped fresh rosemary leaves
- 400 g/14 oz red Camargue rice
- 850 ml/1½ pints hot chicken stock
- 1 red onion
- 1 small carrot, cut into matchsticks
- 1 leek, cut into 1 cm/½ inch rounds
- 85 g/3 oz pine kernels, roasted lightly
- 1 tsp light brown sugar
- 1–2 tbsp chopped fresh coriander
- 150 g/5½ oz dried cranberries, sour cherries or raisins, soaked in boiling water for 15 minutes
- 225 ml/8 fl oz soured cream
- 2 tbsp chopped roasted walnuts, to garnish
- salt and pepper

1 Put about 4 tablespoons of the olive oil in a large bowl and whisk in the orange rind and juice, vinegar, coriander seeds, bay leaf and crushed chillies. Add the beetroots, shallots, parsnips and carrots and stir to coat well.

2 Turn into a roasting tin and roast in a preheated oven at 200°C/400°F/Gas Mark 6 for 45–55 minutes, or until the vegetables are tender, turning occasionally. Remove from the oven, sprinkle with the rosemary and seasoning and keep warm.

3 While the vegetables are cooking, put the red rice in a large saucepan with the hot chicken stock. Place over a medium-high heat and bring to the boil, then reduce the heat to low and simmer, covered, for about 40 minutes, or until the rice is tender and the chicken stock has been absorbed. Remove from the heat, but do not uncover.

4 Heat the remaining oil in a large pan. Add the onion and carrot strips and cook for 8–10 minutes, or until tender. Add the leek, pine kernels, brown sugar and coriander and cook for 2–3 minutes, or until the vegetables are lightly caramelized. Drain the soaked cranberries and stir into the vegetable mixture with the rice. Season with salt and pepper.

5 Arrange the roasted vegetables and rice on a serving platter and top with the soured cream. Sprinkle with the chopped walnuts and serve.

1

2

Curry Patties with Tahini

Substantial and flavourful, these patties are a delicious alternative to beef burgers. Leave the rice with a little bite to give extra texture.

NUTRITIONAL INFORMATION

Calories	335	Sugars	5g
Protein	12g	Fat	22g
Carbohydrate	24g	Saturates	3g

1 ¼ hrs — 35–40 mins

SERVES 4–6

INGREDIENTS

- ½ tsp salt
- 70 g/2½ oz white or brown basmati rice
- 2 tbsp olive oil
- 1 red onion, chopped finely
- 2 garlic cloves
- 2 tsp curry powder
- ½ tsp crushed dried chilli flakes
- 1 small red pepper, cored and diced
- 115 g/4 oz frozen peas, defrosted
- 1 small leek, chopped finely
- 1 ripe tomato, skinned and chopped
- 310 g/11 oz canned chickpeas
- 85 g/3 oz fresh white breadcrumbs
- 1–2 tbsp chopped fresh coriander or mint
- 1 egg, beaten lightly
- vegetable oil, for frying
- salt and pepper

DRESSING

- 125 ml/4 fl oz tahini
- 2 garlic cloves, gently crushed
- ½ tsp ground cumin, or to taste
- pinch of cayenne pepper
- 5 tbsp lemon juice
- drizzle of extra virgin olive oil
- about 125 ml/4 fl oz water

1

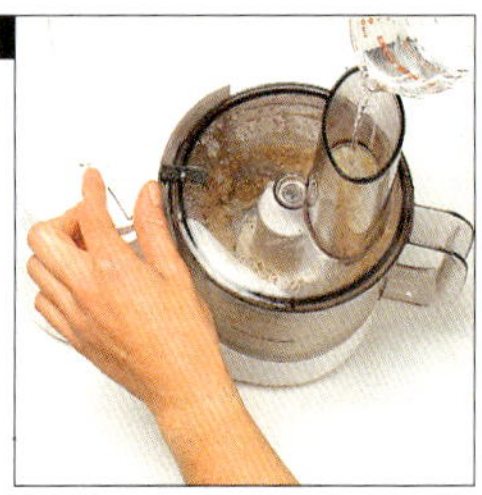

3

1 To make the dressing, blend the tahini, garlic, cumin, cayenne and lemon juice in a food processor until creamy. Slowly pour in the oil, then gradually add water to make a creamy dressing.

2 Bring a saucepan of water to the boil. Add the salt and sprinkle in the rice. Simmer for 15–20 minutes, or until the rice is just tender. Drain, rinse and set aside.

3 Heat the olive oil in a large pan. Add the onion and garlic and cook until they begin to soften. Stir in the curry powder and chilli flakes and cook for 2 minutes. Add the diced pepper, peas, leek and tomato and cook gently for 7 minutes, or until tender. Set aside.

4 Drain and rinse the chickpeas, and process them in the food processor until smooth. Add half the vegetables and process again. Transfer to a large bowl and add the remaining vegetable mixture, breadcrumbs, coriander and egg, and mix well. Stir in the rice and season well. Chill for 1 hour, then shape into 4–6 patties.

5 Fry the patties in oil for 6–8 minutes, or until golden. Garnish with cucumber slices and serve with the tahini dressing and lime wedges.

Spicy Potato & Rice Pilaf

This spicy blend of potatoes, rice and peas may accompany other dishes in a full Indian meal, but is rich enough to serve on its own.

NUTRITIONAL INFORMATION

Calories	217	Sugars	3g
Protein	6g	Fat	4g
Carbohydrate	39g	Saturates	0.1g

5–10 mins   40 mins

SERVES 4–6

INGREDIENTS

- 200 g/7 oz basmati rice, soaked in cold water for 20 minutes
- 2 tbsp vegetable oil
- ½–¾ tsp cumin seeds
- 225 g/8 oz potatoes, cut into 1 cm/½ inch pieces
- 225 g/8 oz frozen peas, defrosted
- 1 green chilli, deseeded and thinly sliced (optional)
- ½ tsp salt
- 1 tsp garam masala
- ½ tsp ground turmeric
- ¼ tsp cayenne pepper
- 600 ml/1 pint water
- 2 tbsp chopped fresh coriander
- 1 red onion, chopped finely
- natural yogurt, to serve

1 Rinse the soaked rice under cold running water until the water runs clear. Drain and set aside.

2 Heat the oil in a large heavy-based saucepan over a medium-high heat. Add the cumin seeds and stir for about 10 seconds until the seeds jump and colour.

3 Add the potatoes, peas and sliced chilli, if using, and stir-fry for about 3 minutes, or until the potatoes are just beginning to soften.

4 Add the rice and cook, stirring frequently, until coated and beginning to turn translucent. Stir in the salt, garam masala, turmeric and cayenne pepper, then add the water. Bring to the boil, stirring once or twice, then reduce the heat to medium and simmer, covered, until most of the water is absorbed and the surface is filled with little steam-holes. Do not stir.

5 Reduce the heat to very low and, if possible, raise the pan about 2.5 cm/1 inch above the heat source by resting on a ring. Cover and steam for about 10 minutes longer. Remove from the heat, uncover and put a clean tea towel or kitchen paper over the rice, and re-cover. Let stand for 5 minutes.

6 Gently fork the rice and potato mixture into a warmed serving bowl and sprinkle with the coriander and chopped red onion. Serve hot with natural yogurt handed separately.

4

5

6

Easy Cheese Risotto

Although this is the easiest, most basic risotto, it is one of the most delicious. Because there are few ingredients, use the best of each.

NUTRITIONAL INFORMATION

Calories	353	Sugars	2g
Protein	10g	Fat	15g
Carbohydrate	40g	Saturates	9g

5 mins · 30–35 mins

SERVES 4–6

INGREDIENTS

- 4–5 tbsp unsalted butter
- 1 onion, chopped finely
- 300 g/10½ oz arborio or carnaroli rice
- 125 ml/4 fl oz dry white vermouth or white wine
- 1.2 litres/2 pints chicken or vegetable stock, simmering
- 85 g/3 oz freshly grated Parmesan cheese, plus extra for sprinkling
- salt and pepper

1 Heat about 2 tablespoons of the butter in a large heavy-based saucepan over a medium heat. Add the onion and cook for about 2 minutes, or until just beginning to soften. Add the rice and cook for 2 minutes, stirring frequently, until translucent and well coated with the butter.

2 Pour in the vermouth: it will bubble and steam rapidly and evaporate almost immediately. Add a ladleful of the simmering stock and cook, stirring constantly, until the stock is absorbed.

3 Continue adding the stock about half a ladleful at a time, letting each addition be absorbed by the rice before adding the next. This should take about 20–25 minutes. The finished risotto should have a creamy consistency and the cooked rice grains should be tender, but still firm to the bite.

4 Remove the pan from the heat and stir the remaining butter and the grated Parmesan cheese into the risotto. Season with salt and a little pepper, to taste. Cover, let stand for about 1 minute, then serve immediately with extra grated Parmesan for sprinkling.

1

3

4

COOK'S TIP

If you prefer not to use butter, soften the onion in 2 tablespoons of olive oil and stir in about 2 tablespoons of extra virgin olive oil with the Parmesan at the end.

Risotto with Asparagus

Using the best asparagus available turns this simple recipe, an Italian classic, into a gourmet treat for lunch or supper.

NUTRITIONAL INFORMATION

Calories	494	Sugars	3g
Protein	15g	Fat	23g
Carbohydrate	61g	Saturates	11g

5–10 mins | 30–35 mins

SERVES 6

I N G R E D I E N T S

- 900 g/2 lb fresh asparagus, washed
- 2 tbsp sunflower or other vegetable oil
- 6 tbsp unsalted butter
- 2 shallots or 1 small onion, chopped finely
- 400 g/14 oz arborio or carnaroli rice
- 1.5 litres/2¾ pints light chicken or vegetable stock, simmering
- 85 g/3 oz freshly grated Parmesan cheese
- salt and pepper
- Parmesan shavings, to garnish (optional)

1

2

6

1 Lightly peel the stems of the asparagus and trim off the woody ends. Cut the tips off each stalk and set them aside, then cut the remaining stems into 2.5 cm/1 inch pieces.

2 Add the asparagus stem pieces to a pan of boiling water and boil for 2 minutes. Add the asparagus tips and boil for about 1 minute, or until tender-crisp. Do not overcook. Rinse under cold running water and set aside.

3 Heat the oil with half the butter in a large heavy-based saucepan. Add the shallots and cook gently for 2 minutes until softened. Add the rice and cook, stirring frequently, for about 2 minutes, until the rice is translucent and well coated.

4 Add a ladleful of the simmering stock and cook, stirring constantly, until the stock is completely absorbed.

5 Continue adding the stock, about half a ladleful at a time, letting each addition be absorbed before adding the next. This should take about 20–25 minutes. The risotto should have a creamy consistency and the rice should be tender, but firm to the bite.

6 Heat the asparagus tips in the stock. Stir the stems into the risotto with the last ladleful of stock, the remaining butter and the grated Parmesan cheese. Remove from the heat, stir in the asparagus tips and season if necessary. Serve with Parmesan shavings, if wished.

Fennel Risotto with Vodka

The alcohol in the vodka cooks out, but leaves a pleasant, tantalizing flavour which complements the cool sweetness of the fennel.

NUTRITIONAL INFORMATION

Calories	385	Sugars	4g
Protein	10g	Fat	10g
Carbohydrate	55g	Saturates	3g

5 mins 30–35 mins

SERVES 4–6

INGREDIENTS

- 2 large fennel bulbs
- 2 tbsp vegetable oil
- 6 tbsp unsalted butter
- 1 large onion, chopped finely
- 350 g/12 oz arborio or carnaroli rice
- 150 ml/5 fl oz vodka (or lemon-flavoured vodka, if you can find it)
- 1.3 litres/2¼ pints light chicken or vegetable stock, simmering
- 55 g/2 oz freshly grated Parmesan cheese
- 5–6 tbsp lemon juice
- salt and pepper

1 Trim the fennel, reserving the fronds for the garnish, if wished. Cut the bulbs in half lengthways, remove the V-shaped cores and roughly chop the flesh. (If you like, add any of the fennel trimmings to the stock for extra flavour.)

2 Heat the oil and half the butter in a large heavy-based saucepan over a medium heat. Add the onion and fennel and cook for about 2 minutes, stirring frequently, until the vegetables are softened. Add the rice and cook for about 2 minutes, stirring frequently, or until the rice is translucent and well coated.

3 Pour in the vodka: it will bubble rapidly and evaporate almost immediately. Add a ladleful of the stock. Cook, stirring constantly, until the stock is absorbed.

4 Continue stirring in the stock, about half a ladleful at a time, letting each addition be absorbed by the rice before adding the next. This should take about 20–25 minutes. The finished risotto should have a creamy consistency, and the rice grains should be just tender, but firm to the bite.

5 Stir in the remaining butter, with the grated Parmesan cheese and lemon juice. Remove from the heat, cover and leave to stand for 1 minute before serving. Garnish with a few of the reserved fennel fronds, if wished.

1

2

5

Roasted Pumpkin Risotto

The combination of sweet creamy pumpkin with the slight saltiness of dolcelatte cheese and the pungency of sage is a delicious surprise.

NUTRITIONAL INFORMATION

Calories	615	Sugars	2g
Protein	19g	Fat	37g
Carbohydrate	53g	Saturates	18g

5–10 mins | 40–45 mins

SERVES 6

INGREDIENTS

- 4 tbsp olive oil
- 4 tbsp unsalted butter, cut into small pieces
- 450 g/1 lb pumpkin flesh, cut into 1 cm/½ inch dice
- ¾ tsp rubbed sage
- 2 garlic cloves, chopped finely
- 2 tbsp lemon juice
- 2 large shallots, chopped finely
- 350 g/12 oz arborio or carnaroli rice
- 50 ml/2 fl oz dry white vermouth
- 1.2 litres/2 pints chicken stock, simmering
- 60 g/2¼ oz freshly grated Parmesan cheese
- 300 g/10½ oz dolcelatte, cut into small pieces
- salt and pepper
- celery leaves, to garnish

1 Put half the olive oil and about 1 tablespoon of the butter in a roasting tin and heat in a preheated oven at 200°C/ 400°F/Gas Mark 6.

2 Add the pumpkin to the tin and sprinkle with the sage, half the garlic and salt and pepper. Toss together and roast for about 10 minutes until just softened and beginning to caramelize. Transfer to a plate.

3 Roughly mash about half the cooked pumpkin with the lemon juice and reserve with the remaining diced pumpkin.

4 Heat the remaining olive oil and 1 tablespoon of the butter in a large heavy-based saucepan over a medium heat. Stir in the chopped shallots and remaining garlic and cook for about 1 minute. Add the rice and cook, stirring, for about 2 minutes, or until well coated.

5 Pour in the vermouth: it will bubble and steam rapidly. Add a ladleful of the simmering stock and cook, stirring constantly, until the liquid is absorbed.

6 Continue adding the stock, about half a ladleful at a time, letting each addition be absorbed before adding the next. This should take about 20–25 minutes. The finished risotto should have a creamy consistency and the rice should be tender, but firm to the bite.

7 Stir all the pumpkin into the risotto with the remaining butter and the grated Parmesan cheese. Remove from the heat and fold in the diced dolcelatte. Serve at once, garnished with celery leaves.

2

7

Wild Rocket Risotto

Search the markets for wild rocket to use in this dish. Its robust, peppery flavour makes all the difference to the taste of the risotto.

NUTRITIONAL INFORMATION	
Calories 546	Sugars 6g
Protein 23g	Fat 24g
Carbohydrate . . 57g	Saturates 12g

5 mins 30–35 mins

SERVES 4–6

INGREDIENTS

- 2 tbsp olive oil
- 2 tbsp unsalted butter
- 1 large onion, chopped finely
- 2 garlic cloves, chopped finely
- 350 g/12 oz arborio rice
- 125 ml/4 fl oz dry white vermouth (optional)
- 1.5 litres/2¾ pints chicken or vegetable stock, simmering
- 6 vine-ripened or Italian plum tomatoes, deseeded and chopped
- 125 g/4½ oz wild rocket
- handful of fresh basil leaves
- 115 g/4 oz freshly grated Parmesan cheese
- 225 g/8 oz fresh Italian buffalo mozzarella, grated roughly or diced
- salt and pepper

1 Heat the oil and half the butter in a large frying pan. Add the onion and cook for 2 minutes, or until just beginning to soften. Add the garlic and rice and cook, stirring, until the rice is well coated.

2 Pour in the white vermouth, if using: it will bubble and evaporate almost immediately. Add a ladleful of the stock and cook, stirring, until it is absorbed.

3 Continue adding the stock, about half a ladleful at a time, letting each addition be absorbed by the rice before adding the next.

4 After about 15 minutes, stir in the chopped plum tomatoes and wild rocket. Shred the fresh basil leaves and immediately stir into the risotto. Continue cooking for about 10 minutes, adding more of the stock, until the risotto takes on a creamy consistency and the rice grains are tender, but firm to the bite.

5 Remove from the heat and stir in the remaining butter, and the Parmesan and mozzarella cheese. Season to taste with salt and pepper. Cover and leave to stand for about 1 minute, then serve, before the mozzarella melts completely.

1

4

5

Frittata Risotto

An excellent way of using up leftover risotto, this fried rice cake makes a great first course, or a tasty accompaniment to roasted or grilled meats.

NUTRITIONAL INFORMATION

Calories	567	Sugars	14g
Protein	14g	Fat	34g
Carbohydrate	50g	Saturates	14g

5 mins 15 mins

SERVES 4–6

INGREDIENTS

- about 80 ml/3 fl oz olive oil
- 1 large red onion, chopped finely
- 1 red pepper, cored, deseeded and chopped
- 1 garlic clove, chopped finely
- 3–4 sun-dried tomatoes, shredded finely
- 2 tbsp chopped fresh flat-leaved parsley or basil
- 1 quantity Easy Cheese Risotto (see page 26), cooled
- about 55 g/2 oz freshly grated Parmesan cheese

1 Heat 2 tablespoons of the olive oil in a large heavy-based frying pan over a medium-high heat. Add the onion and red pepper and cook for 3–4 minutes, or until the vegetables are soft.

2 Add the garlic and shredded sun-dried tomatoes and cook for 2 minutes. Remove from the heat, stir in the parsley and cool slightly.

3 Put the risotto in a bowl and break up with a fork. Stir in the vegetable mixture with half the Parmesan. Mix well.

4 Reserve 1 tablespoon of the remaining olive oil and heat the rest in the cleaned frying pan over a medium heat. Remove from the heat and spoon in the risotto mixture, pressing it into an even, cakelike layer, about 2–2.5 cm/$\frac{3}{4}$–1 inch thick. Return to the heat and cook for about 4 minutes, or until crisp and brown on the bottom.

5 With a palette knife, loosen the edges and give the pan a shake. Slide the frittata on to a large plate. Protecting your hands, invert the frying pan over the frittata and, holding both firmly together, flip them over. Return to the heat and drizzle the remaining oil around the edge of the frittata, gently pulling the edges towards the centre with the palette knife. Cook for 1–2 minutes to seal the bottom, then slide on to a serving plate.

6 Sprinkle the top with some of the remaining Parmesan. Cut into wedges and serve with the rest of the Parmesan.

Stuffed Peppers

Serve these Mediterranean-style peppers with their tops – blanch the tops with the peppers, then bake them separately for the last 10 minutes.

NUTRITIONAL INFORMATION			
Calories	366	Sugars	24g
Protein	12g	Fat	12g
Carbohydrate	54g	Saturates	4g

10 mins 1 hr 25 mins

SERVES 6

INGREDIENTS

- 6 large red, yellow and orange peppers
- 200 g/7 oz long-grain white rice
- 2–3 tbsp olive oil, plus extra for greasing and drizzling
- 1 large onion
- 2 celery sticks, chopped
- 2 garlic cloves, chopped finely
- ½ tsp ground cinnamon or allspice
- 75 g/2¾ oz raisins
- 4 tbsp pine kernels, toasted lightly
- 4 ripe plum tomatoes, deseeded and chopped
- 50 ml/2 fl oz white wine
- 4 anchovy fillets, chopped
- ½ bunch fresh parsley, chopped
- ½ bunch fresh mint, chopped
- 6 tbsp freshly grated Parmesan cheese
- salt and pepper
- fresh tomato sauce, to serve (optional)

1 Using a sharp knife, slice off the tops of the peppers, then remove the cores and seeds. Blanch the peppers in boiling water for 2–3 minutes. Carefully remove and drain upside-down on a wire rack.

2 Bring a saucepan of salted water to the boil. Gradually pour in the rice and return to the boil, then simmer until tender, but firm to the bite. Drain and rinse under cold running water. Set aside.

3 Heat the oil in a large frying pan. Add the onion and celery and cook for 2 minutes. Stir in the garlic, cinnamon and raisins and cook for 1 minute.

4 Fork the rice into the pan, then stir in the pine kernels, tomatoes, wine, anchovies, parsley and mint and cook for 4 minutes. Remove from the heat, season with salt and pepper and stir in half the grated Parmesan cheese.

5 Brush the bottom of a baking dish with a little oil. Divide the rice mixture equally among the peppers. Arrange in the dish and sprinkle with the remaining Parmesan. Drizzle with a little more oil and pour in enough water to come 1 cm/½ inch up the sides of the peppers. Loosely cover the dish with kitchen foil.

6 Bake in a preheated oven, 180°C/350°F/Gas Mark 4, for about 40 minutes. Uncover and cook for a further 10 minutes. Serve hot with tomato sauce.

1

4

5

Sage Chicken & Rice

Cooking in a single pot means that all of the flavours are retained. This is a substantial meal that needs only a salad and some crusty bread.

NUTRITIONAL INFORMATION

Calories	247	Sugars	5g
Protein	26g	Fat	5g
Carbohydrate	25g	Saturates	2g

10 mins — 50 mins

SERVES 4

INGREDIENTS

- 1 large onion, chopped
- 1 garlic clove, crushed
- 2 celery sticks, sliced
- 2 carrots, diced
- 2 sprigs fresh sage
- 300 ml/10 fl oz chicken stock
- 350 g/12 oz boneless, skinless chicken breasts
- 225 g/8 oz mixed brown and wild rice
- 400 g/14 oz canned chopped tomatoes
- dash of Tabasco sauce
- 2 medium courgettes, trimmed and sliced thinly
- 100 g/3½ oz lean ham, diced
- salt and pepper
- fresh sage, to garnish

TO SERVE

- salad leaves
- crusty bread

1 Place the onion, garlic, celery, carrots and sprigs of fresh sage in a large saucepan and pour in the chicken stock. Bring to the boil, cover the pan and simmer for 5 minutes.

2 Cut the chicken into 2.5 cm/1 inch cubes and stir into the pan with the vegetables. Cover the pan and continue to cook for a further 5 minutes.

3 Stir in the mixed brown and wild rice and chopped tomatoes.

4 Add a dash of Tabasco sauce to taste and season well. Bring to the boil, cover and simmer for 25 minutes.

5 Stir in the sliced courgettes and diced ham and continue to cook, uncovered, for 10 minutes, stirring occasionally, until the rice is just tender.

6 Remove the sprigs of fresh sage from the pan and discard. Garnish the dish with sage leaves and serve with plenty of salad leaves and fresh crusty bread.

2

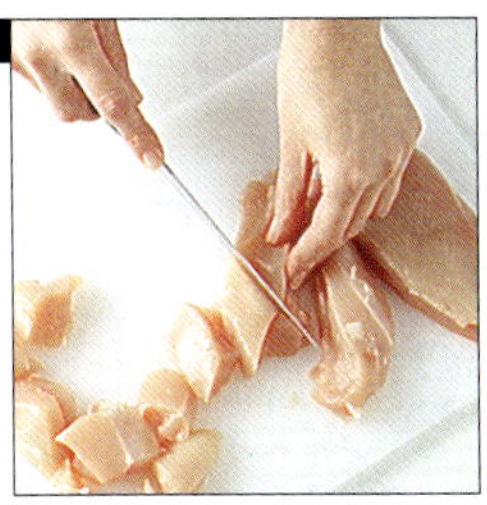

3

5

Orange Turkey with Rice

This is a good way to use up leftover rice. Use fresh or canned sweet pink grapefruit for an interesting alternative to the orange.

NUTRITIONAL INFORMATION			
Calories	337	Sugars	12g
Protein	32g	Fat	7g
Carbohydrate	40g	Saturates	1g

30 mins 40 mins

SERVES 4

INGREDIENTS

- 1 tbsp olive oil
- 1 medium onion, chopped
- 450 g/1 lb skinless lean turkey (such as fillet), cut into thin strips
- 300 ml/10 fl oz unsweetened orange juice
- 1 bay leaf
- 225 g/8 oz small broccoli florets
- 1 large courgette, diced
- 1 large orange
- 350 g/12 oz cooked brown rice
- salt and pepper
- tomato and onion salad, to serve

TO GARNISH

- 25 g/1 oz pitted black olives in brine, drained and quartered
- shredded basil leaves

2

3

4

1 Heat the oil in a large frying pan and fry the onion and turkey, stirring, for 4–5 minutes, or until lightly browned.

2 Pour in the orange juice and add the bay leaf and seasoning. Bring to the boil and simmer for 10 minutes.

3 Meanwhile, bring a large saucepan of water to the boil and cook the broccoli florets, covered, for 2 minutes. Add the diced courgette, bring back to the boil, cover and cook for a further 3 minutes. Do not overcook. Drain and set aside.

4 Using a sharp knife, peel off the skin and white pith from the orange. Thinly slice the orange to make round slices, then halve each slice.

5 Stir the broccoli, courgette, rice and orange slices into the turkey mixture. Gently mix together and season, then heat through for a further 3–4 minutes until piping hot.

6 Transfer the turkey rice to warm serving plates and garnish with black olives and shredded basil leaves. Serve the turkey with a fresh tomato and onion salad.

Cajun Chicken Gumbo

This complete main course is cooked in one saucepan. If you are cooking for one, halve the ingredients – the cooking time should stay the same.

NUTRITIONAL INFORMATION

Calories	425	Sugars	8g
Protein	34g	Fat	12g
Carbohydrate	48g	Saturates	3g

5 mins — 25 mins

SERVES 2

INGREDIENTS

- 1 tbsp sunflower oil
- 4 chicken thighs
- 1 small onion, diced
- 2 celery sticks, diced
- 1 small green pepper, diced
- 85 g/3 oz long-grain rice
- 300 ml/10 fl oz chicken stock
- 1 small red chilli
- 225 g/8 oz okra
- 1 tbsp tomato purée
- salt and pepper

1 Heat the oil in a wide pan and fry the chicken until golden. Remove the chicken from the pan.

2 Put the onion, celery and pepper in the pan and fry for 1 minute. Pour off any excess oil.

3 Add the rice and fry, stirring, for a further minute. Add the chicken stock and bring to a boil. Thinly slice the red chilli and trim the okra, and stir in to the gumbo with the tomato purée. Season to taste with salt and pepper.

4 Return the chicken to the pan and stir. Cover tightly and simmer gently for 15 minutes, or until the rice is tender, the chicken is thoroughly cooked and the liquid absorbed. Stir occasionally and if it becomes too dry, add a little extra stock.

COOK'S TIP

The whole chilli makes the dish hot and spicy – if you prefer a milder flavour, discard the seeds of the chilli.

Chicken Basquaise

This dish is from the Basque region in the west Pyrenees. Bayonne ham, a traditional Pyrenean air-dried meat, adds a delicious flavour.

NUTRITIONAL INFORMATION

Calories	559	Sugars	8g
Protein	50g	Fat	21g
Carbohydrate	44g	Saturates	6g

5–10 mins | 1 hr 20 mins

SERVES 4–5

INGREDIENTS

- 1.3 kg/3 lb chicken, cut into 8 pieces
- flour, for dusting
- 2–3 tbsp olive oil
- 1 large onion (preferably Spanish), thickly sliced
- 2 peppers, deseeded and cut lengthways into thick strips
- 2 garlic cloves
- 150 g/5½ oz spicy chorizo sausage, peeled, if necessary, and cut into 1 cm/½ inch pieces
- 1 tbsp tomato purée
- 200 g/7 oz long-grain white rice or medium-grain Spanish rice, such as Valencia
- 450 ml/16 fl oz chicken stock
- 1 tsp crushed dried chillies
- ½ tsp dried thyme
- 115 g/4 oz Bayonne or other air-dried ham, diced
- 12 dry-cured black olives
- 2 tbsp chopped fresh flat-leaved parsley
- salt and pepper

1 Dry the chicken pieces well with kitchen paper. Put about 2 tablespoons of flour in a plastic bag, season with salt and pepper and add the chicken pieces. Seal the bag and shake to coat the chicken.

2 Heat 2 tablespoons of the oil in a large flameproof casserole over a medium-high heat. Add the chicken and cook for about 15 minutes, or until well browned. Transfer to a plate and set aside.

2

3 Heat the remaining oil in the pan and add the onion and peppers. Reduce the heat to medium and stir-fry until beginning to colour and soften. Add the garlic, chorizo and tomato purée and continue stirring for about 3 minutes. Add the rice and cook for about 2 minutes, stirring to coat, until the rice is translucent.

3

4 Add the stock, crushed chillies, thyme and salt and pepper and stir. Bring to the boil. Return the chicken to the pan, pressing gently into the rice. Cover and cook over a very low heat for about 45 minutes, or until the chicken and rice are tender.

5 Gently stir the ham, black olives and half the parsley into the rice mixture. Re-cover and heat through for a further 5 minutes. Sprinkle with the remaining parsley and serve.

5

Pad Thai

All over Thailand and South East Asia, cooks at streetside and floating food stalls stir-fry these simple, delicious rice noodles to order.

NUTRITIONAL INFORMATION

Calories	527	Sugars	8g
Protein	34g	Fat	17g
Carbohydrate	58g	Saturates	3g

20 mins 10 mins

SERVES 4

INGREDIENTS

- 225 g/8 oz flat rice noodles (sen lek)
- 2 tbsp groundnut or vegetable oil
- 225 g/8 oz boneless chicken breasts, skinned and sliced thinly
- 4 shallots, chopped finely
- 2 garlic cloves, chopped finely
- 4 spring onions, cut on the diagonal into 5 cm/2 inch pieces
- 350 g/12 oz fresh white crab meat
- 75 g/2¾ oz beansprouts, rinsed
- 1 tbsp finely diced preserved radish or fresh radish
- 2–4 tbsp roasted peanuts, chopped
- fresh coriander sprigs, to garnish

SAUCE

- 3 tbsp Thai fish sauce
- 2–3 tbsp rice vinegar or cider vinegar
- 1 tbsp chilli bean sauce or oyster sauce
- 1 tbsp toasted sesame oil
- 1 tbsp palm sugar or light brown sugar
- ½ tsp cayenne pepper or 1 fresh red chilli, thinly sliced

4

5

6

1 To make the sauce, whisk together the sauce ingredients in a small bowl and set aside.

2 Put the rice noodles in a large bowl and pour over enough hot water to cover. Let stand for 15 minutes, or until softened. Drain, rinse and drain again.

3 Heat the oil in a heavy-based wok over a high heat until very hot, but not smoking. Add the chicken and stir-fry for 1–2 minutes or until it begins to colour. Using a slotted spoon, transfer to a plate. Reduce the heat to medium-high.

4 Stir the shallots, garlic and spring onions into the wok and stir-fry for about 1 minute. Stir in the drained noodles, then the prepared sauce.

5 Return the reserved chicken to the pan with the crab meat, beansprouts and radish and toss well. Cook for about 5 minutes until heated through, tossing frequently. If the noodles begin to stick, add a little water.

6 Turn into a serving dish and sprinkle with the chopped peanuts. Garnish with coriander and serve immediately.

Azerbaijani Lamb Pilaf

This type of dish is popular from the Balkans, through Russia and the Middle East to India. Saffron and pomegranate juice give it an exotic air.

NUTRITIONAL INFORMATION

Calories	399	Sugars	19g
Protein	25g	Fat	13g
Carbohydrate	47g	Saturates	4g

5 mins — 45–55 mins

SERVES 4–6

INGREDIENTS

- 2–3 tbsp oil
- 650 g/1 lb 7 oz boneless lamb shoulder, cut into 2.5 cm/1 inch cubes
- 2 onions, roughly chopped
- 1 tsp ground cumin
- 200 g/7 oz arborio, long-grain or basmati rice
- 1 tbsp tomato purée
- 1 tsp saffron threads
- 100 ml/3½ fl oz pomegranate juice (see Cook's Tip)
- 850 ml/1½ pints lamb or chicken stock, or water
- 115 g/4 oz dried apricots or prunes, ready soaked and halved
- 2 tbsp raisins
- salt and pepper
- 4 tbsp mixed chopped fresh watercress and mint, to serve

1 Heat the oil in a large flameproof casserole or wide saucepan over a high heat. Add the lamb in batches and cook for about 7 minutes, turning, until lightly browned all over.

2 Add the onions to the casserole, reduce the heat to medium-high and cook for about 2 minutes, or until beginning to soften. Add the cumin and rice and cook for about 2 minutes, stirring to coat well, until the rice is translucent. Stir in the tomato purée and the saffron threads.

3 Add the pomegranate juice and stock and bring the mixture to the boil, stirring once or twice. Add the soaked apricots or prunes and the raisins to the casserole, then stir to mix well together. Reduce the heat to low, cover, and simmer for about 20–25 minutes, or until the lamb and rice are just tender and the liquid has been absorbed.

4 Sprinkle the chopped watercress and mint over the pilaf and serve straight from the pan.

1

2

3

COOK'S TIP

Pomegranate juice is available from grocery stores selling produce from the Middle East. If you cannot find it, use unsweetened grape or apple juice.

Tomato Rice with Sausages

A quick and filling supper for a young family, this dish is simple to put together and always popular because it tastes so good.

NUTRITIONAL INFORMATION

Calories	708	Sugars	7g
Protein	27g	Fat	35g
Carbohydrate	76g	Saturates	16g

5 mins 45 mins

SERVES 4

INGREDIENTS

- 2 tbsp vegetable oil
- 1 onion, roughly chopped
- 1 red pepper, cored, deseeded and chopped
- 2 garlic cloves, chopped finely
- ½ tsp dried thyme
- 300 g/10½ oz long-grain white rice
- 1 litre/1¾ pints light chicken or vegetable stock
- 225 g/8 oz canned chopped tomatoes
- 1 bay leaf
- 2 tbsp shredded fresh basil
- 175 g/6 oz mature Cheddar cheese, grated
- 2 tbsp chopped fresh chives
- 4 herby pork sausages, cooked and cut into 1 cm/½ inch pieces
- 2–3 tbsp freshly grated Parmesan cheese

1 Heat the oil in a large flame-proof casserole over medium heat. Add the onion and red pepper and cook for about 5 minutes, stirring frequently, until soft and lightly coloured. Stir in the garlic and thyme and cook for a further minute.

2 Add the rice and cook, stirring frequently, for about 2 minutes, or until it is well coated and translucent. Stir in the stock, tomatoes and bay leaf. Boil for 5 minutes, or until the stock has almost been absorbed by the rice.

3 Stir in the basil, Cheddar cheese, chives and pork sausages and bake, covered, in a preheated oven, at 180°C/350°F/Gas Mark 4, for about 25 minutes.

4 Sprinkle with the grated Parmesan cheese and return to the oven, uncovered, for 5 minutes, until the top is golden. Serve hot from the casserole.

2

3

4

VARIATION

For a vegetarian version, replace the pork sausages with 400 g/14 oz canned butter beans, kidney beans or sweetcorn, drained; or try a mixture of sautéed mushrooms and courgettes.

Italian Sausage Risotto

This dish is made with a mild Italian sausage called luganega, but you can use any sausage – a spicy Spanish chorizo would give an unusual flavour.

NUTRITIONAL INFORMATION

Calories	630	Sugars	4g
Protein	19g	Fat	34g
Carbohydrate	57g	Saturates	15g

5 mins — 35–40 mins

SERVES 4–6

INGREDIENTS

- 2 long sprigs fresh rosemary, plus extra to garnish
- 2 tbsp olive oil
- 4 tbsp unsalted butter
- 1 large onion, chopped finely
- 1 celery stick, chopped finely
- 2 garlic cloves, chopped finely
- ½ tsp dried thyme leaves
- 450 g/1 lb pork sausage, such as luganega or Cumberland, cut into 1 cm/½ inch pieces
- 350 g/12 oz arborio or carnaroli rice
- 125 ml/4 fl oz fruity red wine
- 1.3 litres/2¼ pints chicken stock, simmering
- 85 g/3 oz freshly grated Parmesan cheese
- salt and pepper

1 Strip the long thin leaves from the fresh rosemary sprigs, chop finely and set aside.

2 Heat the oil and half the butter in a large heavy-based saucepan over a medium heat. Add the chopped onion and celery and cook for about 2 minutes. Stir in the chopped garlic, dried thyme, sausage and chopped fresh rosemary. Cook for about 5 minutes, stirring frequently, until the sausage begins to brown. Transfer the sausage to a plate.

3 Stir the rice into the pan and cook for about 2 minutes, or until translucent and coated with the butter and oil.

4 Pour in the red wine: it will bubble and steam rapidly and evaporate almost immediately. Add a ladleful of the simmering stock and cook, stirring, until it is absorbed by the rice.

5 Continue adding the stock, about half a ladleful at a time, letting each addition be absorbed before adding the next. This should take about 20–25 minutes. The risotto should have a creamy consistency and the rice should be tender, but firm to the bite.

6 Return the sausage pieces to the risotto and heat through. Remove from the heat and stir in the remaining butter and Parmesan cheese. Season to taste. Cover, let stand for about 1 minute, then garnish with rosemary and serve.

1

2

4

Spanish Paella

This satisfying Mediterranean dish takes its name from the large metal pan traditionally used for cooking it – a *paellera*.

NUTRITIONAL INFORMATION

Calories	1700	Sugars	13g
Protein	103g	Fat	64g
Carbohydrate	181g	Saturates	16g

5 mins

55 mins

SERVES 4

INGREDIENTS

- 125 ml/4 fl oz olive oil
- 1.5 kg/3 lb 5 oz chicken, cut into 8 pieces
- 350 g/12 oz chorizo sausage, cut into 1 cm/½ inch pieces
- 115 g/4 oz cured ham, chopped
- 2 onions, chopped finely
- 2 red peppers, cored, deseeded and cut into 2.5 cm/1 inch pieces
- 4–6 garlic cloves
- 750 g/1 lb 10 oz short-grain Spanish rice or Italian arborio rice
- 2 bay leaves
- 1 tsp dried thyme
- 1 tsp saffron threads, lightly crushed
- 225 ml/8 fl oz dry white wine
- 1.5 litres/2¾ pints chicken stock
- 115 g/4 oz fresh shelled or defrosted frozen peas
- 450 g/1 lb medium uncooked prawns
- 8 raw king prawns, in shells
- 16 clams, very well scrubbed
- 16 mussels, very well scrubbed
- 4 tbsp chopped fresh flat-leaved parsley
- salt and pepper

2

5

1 Heat half the oil in a 46-cm/18-inch paella pan or deep, wide frying pan over a medium-high heat. Add the chicken and fry gently, turning, until golden brown. Remove from the pan and set aside.

2 Add the chopped chorizo and ham to the pan and cook for about 7 minutes, stirring occasionally, until crisp. Remove and set aside.

3 Stir the onions into the pan and cook for about 3 minutes until soft. Add the peppers and garlic, cook until beginning to soften, then remove and set aside.

4 Add the remaining oil to the pan and stir in the rice until well coated. Add the bay leaves, thyme and saffron and stir well. Pour in the wine, bubble, then pour in the stock, stirring well and scraping the bottom of the pan. Bring to the boil, stirring the rice frequently.

5 Stir in the cooked vegetables. Add the chorizo, ham and chicken and gently bury them in the rice. Reduce the heat and cook for 10 minutes, stirring occasionally.

6 Add the peas and prawns and cook for a further 5 minutes. Push the clams and mussels into the rice. Cover and cook over a very low heat for about 5 minutes until the rice is tender and the shellfish open. Discard any unopened clams or mussels. Season to taste.

7 Remove from heat, and stand, covered, for about 5 minutes. Sprinkle with parsley and serve.

Creole Jambalaya

This rice-based stew, an extraordinary mix of seafood and meat with exciting peppery flavourings, captures the essence of Creole cooking.

NUTRITIONAL INFORMATION

Calories	424	Sugars	8g
Protein	31g	Fat	11g
Carbohydrate	54g	Saturates	2g

10 mins | 45 mins

SERVES 6–8

INGREDIENTS

- 2 tbsp vegetable oil
- 85 g/3 oz good-quality smoked ham
- 85 g/3 oz andouille or pure smoked pork sausage, such as Polish kielbasa
- 225 g/8 oz skinned, boned chicken breast
- 2 large onions, chopped finely
- 3–4 celery sticks, chopped finely
- 2 green peppers, deseeded and chopped
- 2 garlic cloves, chopped finely
- 4 ripe tomatoes, skinned and chopped
- 175 ml/6 fl oz passata
- 450 ml/16 fl oz fish stock
- 400 g/14 oz long-grain white rice
- 4 spring onions, cut into 2.5 cm/1 inch pieces
- 250 g/9 oz peeled raw prawns, tails on
- 250 g/9 oz cooked white crab meat
- 12 oysters, shelled, with their liquor

SEASONING MIX

- 2 dried bay leaves
- 1 tsp salt
- 1½–2 tsp cayenne pepper, or to taste
- 1½ tsp dried oregano
- 1 tsp ground white pepper, or to taste
- 1 tsp black pepper, or to taste

1. To make the seasoning mix, combine the ingredients in a bowl.

2. Chop the ham, sausage and chicken into bite-sized pieces. Set aside the chicken. Heat the oil in a flameproof casserole over a medium heat. Add the ham and sausage and cook for 8 minutes, stirring, until golden. Using a slotted spoon, transfer to a large plate.

3. Add the onions, celery and peppers to the casserole and cook for about 4 minutes, or until just softened. Stir in the garlic, then remove and set aside.

4. Add the chicken pieces to the casserole and cook for 3–4 minutes. Stir in the seasoning mix to coat.

5. Return the cooked ham, sausage and vegetables to the casserole and stir to combine. Add the chopped tomatoes, passata and stock. Bring to the boil.

6. Stir in the rice and reduce the heat to a simmer. Cook for about 12 minutes. Uncover, stir in the spring onions and prawns and cook, covered, for 4 minutes.

7. Add the crab meat and oysters with their liquor and gently stir in. Cook until the rice is just tender, and the oysters slightly firm. Remove the casserole from the heat and let stand, covered, for about 3 minutes before serving.

3

5

Murgh Pullau

Traditionally, the meat and rice in this dish are cooked together for ease of preparation. Here they are cooked separately to ensure perfect timing.

NUTRITIONAL INFORMATION

Calories	850	Sugars	14g
Protein	44g	Fat	47g
Carbohydrate	63g	Saturates	20g

10 mins 1 hr 5 mins

SERVES 4–6

INGREDIENTS

- 350 g/12 oz basmati rice
- 4 tbsp ghee or butter
- 115 g/4 oz flaked almonds
- 85 g/3 oz unsalted, shelled pistachio nuts
- 4–6 boned chicken breasts, skinned and each cut into 4 pieces
- 2 onions, thinly sliced
- 2 garlic cloves, chopped finely
- 2 tsp chopped fresh root ginger
- 6 green cardamom pods, lightly crushed
- 4–6 whole cloves
- 2 bay leaves
- 1 tsp ground coriander
- ½ tsp cayenne pepper
- 225 ml/8 fl oz natural yogurt
- 225 ml/8 fl oz double cream
- 2–4 tbsp chopped fresh coriander or mint
- 225 g/8 oz seedless green grapes, halved if large

1 Bring a pan of salted water to the boil. Gradually pour in the rice, return to the boil, then simmer until just tender. Drain and rinse under cold running water and set aside.

2 Heat the ghee in a deep frying pan over a medium-high heat. Add the almonds and pistachios and cook for 3 minutes, stirring, until light golden. Remove and reserve.

3 Add the chicken to the pan and cook for about 5 minutes, turning, until golden. Remove and reserve. Add the onions to the pan. Cook for about 10 minutes, until golden. Stir in the garlic and spices and cook for 3 minutes.

4 Add 2–3 tablespoons of the yogurt and cook, stirring, until all the moisture evaporates. Continue adding the rest of the yogurt in the same way.

5 Return the chicken and nuts to the pan and stir to coat. Stir in 125 ml/4 fl oz boiling water. Season with salt and pepper and cook, covered, over a low heat for about 10 minutes, or until the chicken is cooked through. Stir in the cream, coriander and grapes and remove from the heat.

6 Fork the rice into a bowl, then gently fold in the chicken and sauce. Let stand for 5 minutes, then serve.

3

4

6

Lamb Biryani

For an authentic finishing touch, garnish with crisply fried onion rings, toasted flaked almonds, chopped pistachios and edible silver foil (vark).

NUTRITIONAL INFORMATION

Calories	668	Sugars	16g
Protein	41g	Fat	35g
Carbohydrate	78g	Saturates	15g

$2\frac{1}{4}$–$3\frac{1}{4}$ hrs

45 mins

SERVES 6–8

INGREDIENTS

- 900 g/2 lb boned lean leg or shoulder of lamb, cut into 2.5 cm/1 inch cubes
- 6 garlic cloves, chopped finely
- 3 tsp finely chopped fresh root ginger
- 1 tbsp ground cinnamon
- 1 tbsp green cardamom pods, crushed
- 1 tsp whole cloves
- 2 tsp coriander seeds, crushed
- 2 tsp cumin seeds, crushed
- ½ tsp ground turmeric (optional)
- 2 green chillies, deseeded and chopped
- grated rind and juice of 1 lime
- 2 tbsp finely chopped fresh coriander
- 2 tbsp finely chopped fresh mint
- 125 ml/4 fl oz natural yogurt
- 115 g/4 oz ghee, butter or vegetable oil
- 4 onions, 3 thinly sliced, 1 chopped finely
- 600 g/1 lb 5 oz basmati rice
- 2 cinnamon sticks, broken
- ½ a whole nutmeg
- 3–4 tbsp raisins
- 1.2 litres/2 pints chicken stock or water
- 225 ml/8 fl oz hot milk
- 1 tsp saffron threads, slightly crushed
- salt and pepper

2

3

1 Combine the lamb with the garlic, ginger, ground cinnamon, cardamom, cloves, coriander and cumin seeds, turmeric, chillies, lime rind and juice, fresh coriander, mint and yogurt and marinate the spiced meat for 2–3 hours.

2 Heat about half the fat in a large frying pan, add the sliced onions, and cook for about 8 minutes, or until they are lightly browned. Add the spiced meat and any juices; season with salt and pepper. Stir in about 225 ml/8 fl oz water and simmer for 18–20 minutes, or until just cooked.

3 Meanwhile, heat the fat left over in a flameproof casserole. Add the chopped onion and cook for 2 minutes, or until soft. Add the rice and cook, stirring constantly, for 3–4 minutes until well coated. Add the cinnamon sticks, nutmeg, raisins and stock. Bring to the boil, stirring once or twice, and season with salt and pepper. Simmer, the rice, covered, over a low heat for 12 minutes, or until the liquid is reduced but the grains are still firm.

4 Pour the hot milk over the saffron and let it stand for 10 minutes. Remove the rice from the heat and stir in the saffron-flavoured milk. Fold in the lamb mixture. Cover and bake in a preheated oven, at 350°C/180°F/Gas Mark 4, until the rice is cooked and the liquid absorbed.

Red Pork Curry

Thai food has become so popular in recent years that most ingredients can be found in your local supermarket.

NUTRITIONAL INFORMATION

Calories	398	Sugars	12g
Protein	38g	Fat	9g
Carbohydrate	47g	Saturates	3g

10 mins — 45 mins

SERVES 4–6

INGREDIENTS

- 900 g/2 lb boned pork shoulder, thinly sliced
- 3 cups coconut milk
- 2 red chillies, deseeded and thinly sliced
- 2 tbsp Thai fish sauce
- 2 tsp brown sugar
- 1 large red pepper, deseeded and sliced
- 6 kaffir lime leaves, shredded
- ½ bunch fresh mint leaves, shredded
- ½ bunch Thai or ordinary basil leaves
- Thai fragrant rice, cooked according to the packet instructions and kept warm

RED CURRY PASTE

- 1 tsp salt, or to taste
- 1 tbsp coriander seeds
- 2 tsp cumin seeds
- 2 tsp black or white peppercorns
- 5–8 dried hot red chillies
- 3–4 shallots, chopped
- 6–8 garlic cloves
- 4 tsp chopped fresh galangal or root ginger
- 2 tsp kaffir lime zest or 2 fresh lime leaves, chopped
- 1 tbsp ground red chilli powder
- 1 tbsp shrimp paste
- 2 stalks lemon grass, thinly sliced

1 To make the curry paste, grind the salt, coriander and cumin seeds and peppercorns to a powder. Add the chillies, one by one, to taste, until ground.

2 Put the shallots, garlic, galangal, kaffir lime rind, chilli powder and shrimp paste in a food processor. Process for about 1 minute. Add the ground spices and process again. Adding water, a few drops at a time, continue to process until a thick paste forms. Scrape this into a bowl and stir in the lemon grass.

3 Put about half the red curry paste in a large deep heavy-based frying pan with the pork. Cook over a medium heat for 2–3 minutes, stirring gently, until the pork is evenly coated and begins to brown.

4 Stir in the coconut milk and bring to the boil. Cook, stirring frequently, for about 10 minutes. Reduce the heat, stir in the chillies, Thai fish sauce and brown sugar, and simmer for about 20 minutes. Add the red pepper and simmer for an additional 10 minutes.

5 Add the lime leaves and half the mint and basil to the curry. Transfer to a serving dish, sprinkle with the remaining mint and basil, and serve with the rice.

3

4

Nasi Goreng

This enticing variation on fried rice is bursting with the exotic flavours of Indonesian cooking. It makes a cheering supper dish on a winter evening.

NUTRITIONAL INFORMATION

Calories	504	Sugars	8g
Protein	49g	Fat	15g
Carbohydrate	47g	Saturates	4g

10–15 mins 20 mins

SERVES 4

INGREDIENTS

- 1 large onion, chopped
- 2–3 garlic cloves
- 1 tsp shrimp paste
- 2 red chillies, deseeded and chopped
- vegetable oil
- 3 eggs, lightly beaten
- 450 g/1 lb beef rump steak, about 1 cm/½ inch thick
- 2 carrots, cut into matchsticks
- 175 g/6 oz Chinese long beans or green beans, cut into 2.5 cm/1 inch pieces
- 6 small spring onions, cut into 1 cm/½ inch pieces
- 250 g/9 oz raw shelled prawns
- 750 g/1 lb 10 oz cooked long-grain white rice, at room temperature
- 6 tbsp dark soy sauce

TO GARNISH

- 4 tbsp ready-fried onion flakes
- 10 cm/4 inch piece cucumber, deseeded and cut into matchsticks
- 2 tbsp chopped fresh coriander

3

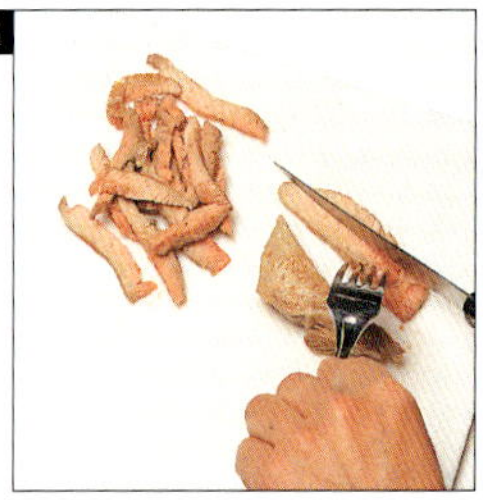

4

1 Put the onion, garlic, shrimp paste and chillies into a food processor and process until a paste forms. Add a little oil and process until smooth. Set aside.

2 Heat 1–2 tablespoons of oil in a large, non-stick frying pan. Pour in the egg to form a thin layer and cook for 1 minute until just set. Turn and cook for 5 seconds on the other side. Slide out and cut in half. Roll up each half, then slice into 5 mm/¼ inch wide strips. Set aside.

3 Heat 2 tablespoons of oil in the same pan over a high heat and add the steak. Cook for 2 minutes on each side to brown and seal. Cool, cut into strips and reserve.

4 Heat 2 tablespoons of oil in a large wok over a medium-high heat. Add the reserved chilli paste and cook, stirring frequently, for about 3 minutes. Add 2 tablespoons of oil, the carrots and long beans. Stir-fry for about 2 minutes. Add the spring onions, prawns and beef strips and stir-fry until the prawns are pink.

5 Stir in the rice, half the sliced omelette, 2 tablespoons of soy sauce and 50 ml/2 fl oz water. Cover and steam for 1 minute. Spoon into a serving dish, top with the remaining omelette and drizzle with the remaining soy sauce. Sprinkle with the onion flakes, cucumber and chopped coriander and serve.

Chinese Fried Rice

This simple Cantonese recipe for using leftover rice has become a speciality of restaurants in Chinatowns the world over.

NUTRITIONAL INFORMATION

Calories	698	Sugars	5g
Protein	29g	Fat	17g
Carbohydrate	115g	Saturates	4g

10 mins   5–10 mins

SERVES 4–6

INGREDIENTS

- 2–3 tbsp groundnut or vegetable oil
- 2 onions, halved and cut lengthways into thin wedges
- 2 garlic cloves, thinly sliced
- 2.5 cm/1 inch piece fresh root ginger, peeled, sliced and cut into slivers
- 200 g/7 oz cooked ham, thinly sliced
- 750 g/1 lb 10 oz cooked, cold long-grain white rice
- 250 g/9 oz cooked peeled prawns
- 115 g/4 oz canned water chestnuts, sliced
- 3 eggs
- 3 tsp sesame oil
- 4–6 spring onions, diagonally sliced into 2.5 cm/1 inch pieces
- 2 tbsp dark soy sauce or Thai fish sauce
- 1 tbsp sweet chilli sauce
- 2 tbsp chopped fresh coriander or flat-leaved parsley
- salt and pepper

1 Heat 2–3 tablespoons of groundnut oil in a wok or large, deep frying pan until very hot. Add the onions and stir-fry for about 2 minutes, or until beginning to soften. Add the garlic and ginger and stir-fry for another minute. Add the ham strips and stir to combine.

2 Add the cold cooked rice and stir to mix with the vegetables and ham. Stir in the prawns and water chestnuts. Stir in 2 tablespoons of water and cover the pan quickly. Continue cooking for 2 minutes to let the rice heat through, shaking the pan occasionally to prevent sticking.

3 Beat the eggs with 1 teaspoon of the sesame oil and season with salt and pepper. Make a well in the centre of the rice mixture, add the eggs and immediately stir, gradually drawing the rice into the eggs.

4 Add the spring onions, soy sauce and chilli sauce and stir-fry, stirring in a little more water if the rice looks dry or is sticking. Drizzle in the remaining sesame oil and stir. Season to taste with salt and pepper.

5 Remove from the heat, wipe the edge of the wok or frying pan and sprinkle with the coriander. Serve immediately from the pan.

2

3

4

Rice with Seafood

This souplike main-course rice dish is packed with fresh seafood, and is typically Thai in flavour.

NUTRITIONAL INFORMATION

Calories	370	Sugars	0g
Protein	27g	Fat	8g
Carbohydrate	52g	Saturates	1g

5–10 mins 20 mins

SERVES 4

INGREDIENTS

- 12 mussels in their shells, cleaned
- 2 litres/3½ pints fish stock
- 2 tbsp vegetable oil
- 1 garlic clove, crushed
- 1 tsp grated fresh root ginger
- 1 red bird-eye chilli, chopped
- 2 spring onions, chopped
- 225 g/8 oz long-grain rice
- 2 small squid, cleaned and sliced
- 100 g/3½ oz firm white fish fillet, such as halibut or monkfish, cut into chunks
- 100 g/3½ oz raw prawns, peeled
- 2 tbsp Thai fish sauce
- 3 tbsp shredded fresh coriander

1 Discard any mussels with damaged shells or open ones that do not close when firmly tapped. Heat 4 tablespoons of the stock in a large pan. Add the mussels, cover and shake the pan until the mussels open. Remove from the heat and discard any which do not open.

2 Heat the oil in a large frying pan or wok and fry the garlic, ginger, chilli and spring onions for 30 seconds. Add the stock and bring to the boil.

3 Stir in the rice, then add the squid, fish chunks and prawns. Lower the heat and simmer gently for 15 minutes, or until the rice is cooked. Add the Thai fish sauce and cooked mussels.

4 Ladle into wide bowls and sprinkle with coriander, before serving.

COOK'S TIP

You could use leftover cooked rice for this dish. Just simmer the seafood gently until cooked, then stir in the rice at the end.

Mixed Seafood Brochettes

If your fishmonger sells turbot steaks, you will probably need one large steak for this dish. Remove the skin and bones and chop the flesh.

NUTRITIONAL INFORMATION

Calories	455	Sugars	0.1g
Protein	32g	Fat	20g
Carbohydrate	39g	Saturates	9g

2¼ hrs — 20 mins

SERVES 4

INGREDIENTS

- 225 g/8 oz skinless, boneless turbot fillet
- 225 g/8 oz skinless, boneless salmon fillet
- 8 scallops
- 8 large tiger prawns or langoustines
- 16 fresh bay leaves
- 1 lemon, sliced
- 4 tbsp olive oil
- grated rind of 1 lemon
- 4 tbsp chopped mixed herbs such as thyme, parsley, chives and basil
- black pepper

LEMON BUTTER RICE

- 175 g/6 oz long-grain rice
- grated rind and juice of 1 lemon
- 4 tbsp butter
- salt and pepper

TO GARNISH

- lemon wedges
- dill sprigs

1 

3 

4 

1 Chop each fish fillet into 8 pieces. Thread on to 8 skewers with the scallops and prawns, alternating with bay leaves and lemon slices. Put into a non-metallic dish in a single layer if possible.

2 Mix together the olive oil, lemon rind, herbs and black pepper. Pour the mixture over the fish. Cover and let marinate for 2 hours, turning once or twice.

3 To make the lemon butter rice, bring a large pan of salted water to the boil and add the rice and grated lemon rind. Return to the boil, then simmer for 7–8 minutes, or until the rice is just tender. Drain well and immediately stir in the lemon juice and butter. Season with salt and pepper to taste.

4 Meanwhile, lift the fish brochettes from their marinade and cook on a lit barbecue or under a preheated hot grill for 8–10 minutes, turning regularly, until cooked through. Serve with lemon butter rice. Garnish with lemon wedges and dill.

A Modern Kedgeree

This modern version of the classic dish uses fresh and smoked salmon and lots of fresh herbs. As a dinner party starter, it would serve six people.

NUTRITIONAL INFORMATION			
Calories	370	Sugars	3g
Protein	10g	Fat	19g
Carbohydrate	39g	Saturates	9g

5 mins

30–35 mins

SERVES 4

INGREDIENTS

- 2 tbsp butter
- 1 tbsp olive oil
- 1 onion, chopped finely
- 1 garlic clove, chopped finely
- 175 g g/6 oz long-grain rice
- 400 ml/14 fl oz fish stock
- 175 g/6 oz skinless, boneless salmon fillet, chopped
- 85 g/3 oz smoked salmon, chopped
- 2 tbsp double cream
- 2 tbsp chopped fresh dill
- 3 spring onions, chopped finely
- salt and pepper
- lemon slices and fresh dill, to garnish

1 Melt the butter with the oil in a large saucepan. Add the onion and cook gently for 10 minutes, or until softened but not coloured. Add the garlic and cook for a further 30 seconds.

2 Add the rice and cook for 2–3 minutes, stirring, until transparent and well coated with oil. Add the fish stock and stir well. Bring to the boil, cover and simmer very gently for 10 minutes.

3 Add the salmon fillet and the smoked salmon and stir well, adding a little more stock or water if it seems dry. Return to the heat and cook for a further 6–8 minutes until the fish and rice are tender and all the stock is absorbed.

4 Remove from the heat and stir in the cream, dill and spring onions. Season to taste and serve immediately, garnished with a sprig of dill and slice of lemon.

COOK'S TIP

Use smoked salmon trimmings for a budget dish.

Jambalaya

Jambalaya is a dish of Cajun origin. There are as many versions of this dish as there are people who cook it.

NUTRITIONAL INFORMATION

Calories	283	Sugars	8g
Protein	30g	Fat	14g
Carbohydrate	12g	Saturates	3g

5 mins — 40–45 mins

SERVES 4

INGREDIENTS

- 2 tbsp vegetable oil
- 2 onions, roughly chopped
- 1 green pepper, deseeded and roughly chopped
- 2 celery sticks, roughly chopped
- 3 garlic cloves, chopped finely
- 2 tsp paprika
- 300 g/10½ oz skinless, boneless chicken breasts, chopped
- 100 g/3½ oz kabanos sausages, chopped
- 3 tomatoes, skinned and chopped
- 450 g/1 lb long-grain rice
- 850 ml/1½ pints hot chicken or fish stock
- 1 tsp dried oregano
- 2 fresh bay leaves
- 12 large prawn tails
- 4 spring onions, chopped finely
- 2 tbsp chopped fresh parsley
- salt and pepper
- salad, to serve

1 Heat the vegetable oil in a large frying pan and add the onions, pepper, celery and garlic. Cook for 8–10 minutes until soft. Add the paprika and cook for another 30 seconds. Add the chicken and sausages and cook for 8–10 minutes, or until lightly browned. Add the tomatoes to the mixture and cook for 2–3 minutes, until collapsed.

2 Add the rice to the pan and stir well. Pour in the hot stock, oregano and bay leaves and stir well. Cover and simmer for 10 minutes over a very low heat.

3 Add the prawns and stir well. Cover again and continue cooking for a further 6–8 minutes until the rice is tender and the prawns are cooked through.

4 Stir in the spring onions and parsley and season to taste. Serve immediately.

Prawn & Asparagus Risotto

This unusual and striking dish with fresh prawns and asparagus is very simple to prepare and ideal for impromptu supper parties.

NUTRITIONAL INFORMATION

Calories	566	Sugars	4g
Protein	30g	Fat	14g
Carbohydrate	86g	Saturates	2g

5 mins 40–45 mins

SERVES 4

INGREDIENTS

- 1.2 litres/2 pints vegetable stock
- 350 g/12 oz asparagus, cut into 5 cm/2 inch lengths
- 2 tbsp olive oil
- 1 onion, chopped finely
- 1 garlic clove, chopped finely
- 350 g/12 oz arborio rice
- 450 g/1 lb raw tiger prawns, peeled and deveined
- 2 tbsp olive paste or tapenade
- 2 tbsp chopped fresh basil
- salt and pepper
- Parmesan cheese shavings, to garnish

1 Bring the vegetable stock to the boil in a large saucepan. Add the asparagus and cook for 3 minutes until just tender. Strain, reserving the stock and keeping it on a low heat. Refresh the asparagus under cold running water. Drain and set aside.

2 Heat the oil in a large frying pan, add the onion and cook gently for 5 minutes, or until softened. Add the garlic and cook for a further 30 seconds. Add the rice and stir for 1–2 minutes, or until coated with the oil and slightly translucent.

3 Raise the heat under the frying pan to medium and add a ladleful of the simmering vegetable stock, stirring the rice until the liquid is absorbed. Continue stirring in the stock, about half a ladleful at a time, letting each be absorbed before adding the next. This should take 20–25 minutes. Add the prawns and asparagus with the last ladleful of stock.

4 Cook for an additional 5 minutes until the prawns and rice are tender and the stock has been absorbed, then remove the pan from the heat.

5 Stir in the olive paste, chopped basil and seasoning and let stand for 1 minute, then serve, garnished with Parmesan cheese shavings.

Coconut Rice with Monkfish

A Thai-influenced dish of rice, cooked in coconut milk, with spicy grilled monkfish and fresh peas.

NUTRITIONAL INFORMATION

Calories	440	Sugars	8g
Protein	22g	Fat	14g
Carbohydrate	60g	Saturates	2g

25 mins | 30–35 mins

SERVES 4

INGREDIENTS

- 1 hot red chilli, deseeded and chopped
- 1 tsp crushed chilli flakes
- 2 garlic cloves, chopped
- 2 pinches saffron
- 3 tbsp roughly chopped mint leaves
- 4 tbsp olive oil
- 2 tbsp lemon juice
- 350 g/12 oz monkfish fillet, cut into bite-sized pieces
- 1 onion, chopped finely
- 225 g/8 oz long grain rice
- 400g/14 oz canned chopped tomatoes
- 200 ml/7 fl oz coconut milk
- 115 g/4 oz peas
- salt and pepper
- 2 tbsp chopped fresh coriander, to garnish

2

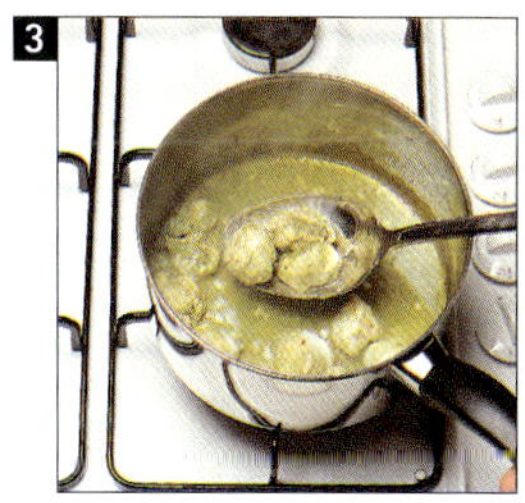

3

4

1 In a food processor or a blender, blend together the fresh chilli, chilli flakes, garlic, saffron, fresh mint, olive oil and lemon juice until the mixture is chopped finely but not smooth.

2 Put the monkfish into a non-metallic dish and pour the spice paste over it, mixing together well. Set aside for 20 minutes to marinate.

3 Heat a large saucepan until it is very hot. Using a slotted spoon, lift the monkfish from the marinade and add it in batches to the hot pan. Cook the fish for 3–4 minutes, or until it is browned and firm. Remove from the pan with a slotted spoon and set it aside.

4 Add the onion and the remaining marinade to the same pan, and cook for 5 minutes, or until softened and lightly browned. Add the rice and stir until well coated. Add the tomatoes and coconut milk. Bring to the boil, cover and simmer very gently for 15 minutes. Stir in the peas, season and arrange the fish over the top. Cover with foil and continue cooking over a very low heat for 5 minutes. Serve garnished with the chopped coriander.

Crab & Pepper Risotto

A different way to make the most of crab, this rich-tasting and colourful risotto is full of interesting flavours.

NUTRITIONAL INFORMATION

Calories	447	Sugars	11g
Protein	22g	Fat	13g
Carbohydrate	62g	Saturates	2g

10–15 mins

30–35 mins

SERVES 4–6

INGREDIENTS

- 2–3 large red peppers
- 3 tbsp olive oil
- 1 onion, chopped finely
- 1 small fennel bulb, chopped finely
- 2 celery sticks, chopped finely
- ¼–½ tsp cayenne pepper, or to taste
- 350 g/12 oz arborio or carnaroli rice
- 800 g/1 lb 12 oz canned Italian peeled plum tomatoes, drained and chopped
- 50 ml/2 fl oz dry white vermouth (optional)
- 1.5 litres/2¾ pints fish or light chicken stock, simmering
- 450 g/1 lb fresh cooked crab meat (white and dark meat)
- 50 ml/2 fl oz lemon juice
- 2–4 tbsp chopped fresh parsley or chervil
- salt and pepper

1 Grill the peppers until the skins are charred. Transfer to a plastic bag and twist to seal. When cool enough to handle, peel off the charred skins, working over a bowl to catch the juices. Remove the cores and seeds. Chop the flesh and set aside, reserving the juices.

2 Heat the olive oil in a large heavy-based saucepan. Add the onion, fennel and celery and cook for 2–3 minutes, or until the vegetables are softened. Add the cayenne and rice and cook, stirring frequently, for about 2 minutes, or until the rice is translucent and well coated.

3 Stir in the tomatoes and vermouth, if using: the liquid will bubble and steam rapidly. When the liquid is almost absorbed, add a ladleful of the simmering stock. Cook, stirring constantly, until the liquid is completely absorbed.

4 Continue adding the stock, about half a ladleful at a time, letting each addition be absorbed before adding the next. This should take about 20–25 minutes. The risotto should have a creamy consistency and the rice should be tender, but firm to the bite.

5 Stir in the red peppers and juices, the crab meat, lemon juice and parsley and heat. Season with salt and pepper to taste. Serve immediately.

1

3

5

Rich Lobster Risotto

Although lobster is expensive, this dish is worth it. Keeping it simple allows the lobster flavour to come through.

NUTRITIONAL INFORMATION

Calories	688	Sugars	3g
Protein	32g	Fat	31g
Carbohydrate	69g	Saturates	16g

5 mins

30–35 mins

SERVES 4

INGREDIENTS

- 1 tbsp vegetable oil
- 4 tbsp unsalted butter
- 2 shallots, chopped finely
- 300 g/10½ oz arborio or carnaroli rice
- ½ tsp cayenne pepper, or to taste
- 80 ml/3 fl oz dry white vermouth
- 1.5 litres/2¾ pints shellfish, fish or light chicken stock, simmering
- 225 g/8 oz cherry tomatoes, quartered and deseeded
- 2–3 tbsp double or whipping cream
- 450 g/1 lb cooked lobster meat, roughly cut into chunks
- 2 tbsp chopped fresh chervil or dill
- salt and white pepper

1

4

5

1 Heat the oil and half the butter in a large heavy-based saucepan over a medium heat. Add the chopped shallots and cook them for about 2 minutes, or until they just begin to soften. Add the rice and the cayenne pepper, and cook, stirring frequently, for about 2 minutes, or until the rice is translucent and well coated with the oil and butter mixture.

2 Pour in the vermouth: it will bubble and steam rapidly and evaporate almost immediately. Add a ladleful of the simmering stock and cook, stirring constantly, until the liquid is absorbed.

3 Continue adding the stock, about half a ladleful at a time, letting each addition be absorbed by the rice before adding the next. Adding all of the stock should take about 20–25 minutes. The finished risotto should have a creamy consistency and the rice should be tender, but still firm to the bite.

4 Stir in the tomatoes and cream and cook for about 2 minutes.

5 Add the cooked lobster meat, with the remaining butter and chervil, and cook long enough to just heat the lobster meat through gently. Serve immediately.

Kedgeree

Originally served at Victorian breakfast tables, kedgeree probably derives from an Indian dish called *khichri*.

NUTRITIONAL INFORMATION

Calories	441	Sugars	2g
Protein	32g	Fat	16g
Carbohydrate	43g	Saturates	7g

15 mins   35–40 mins

SERVES 4–6

INGREDIENTS

- 700 g/1 lb 9 oz thick, undyed smoked haddock or cod fillets
- milk, for poaching
- 2 bay leaves
- 1 tbsp vegetable oil
- 4 tbsp butter
- 1 onion, chopped finely
- 1 tsp hot curry powder, or to taste
- 1 tsp dry mustard powder
- 300 g/10½ oz basmati rice
- 750 ml/1⅓ pints water
- 2 small leeks, trimmed and cut into 5 mm/¼ inch slices
- 2 tbsp chopped fresh flat-leaved parsley or coriander
- a squeeze of lemon juice
- 3–4 hard-boiled eggs, peeled and quartered
- salt and pepper
- lemon quarters, to serve

1 Put the fish in a frying pan, pour in enough milk to just cover and add the bay leaves. Bring to the boil, then simmer gently, covered, for about 4 minutes. Remove from the heat and let stand, covered, for about 10 minutes.

2 Using a slotted spoon, transfer the fish to a plate and cover loosely. Set aside. Reserve the cooking milk, discarding the bay leaves.

3 Heat the oil and half the butter in a flameproof casserole over a medium heat. Add the onion and cook for about 2 minutes, or until soft. Stir in the curry powder and mustard powder and cook for 1 minute.

4 Add the rice and stir for about 2 minutes, or until well coated. Add the water and bring to the boil. Stir, and reduce the heat to very low. Cook, covered, for 20–25 minutes, until the rice is tender and the water absorbed.

5 Melt the remaining butter in a large pan, add the leeks and cook for about 4 minutes, or until soft. Fork the leeks into the hot rice. Add 2–3 tablespoons of the reserved milk to moisten.

6 Flake the fish off the skin into large pieces and fold into the rice. Stir in the fresh parsley or coriander and the lemon juice, then season with salt and pepper. Add a little more milk, if wished, then add the egg quarters. Serve the kedgeree with lemon quarters.

1

5

6

Salmon Coulibiac

Coulibiac is probably the world's tastiest fish pie. It was first made in the 19th century by French chefs working in the Imperial Russian courts.

NUTRITIONAL INFORMATION			
Calories	659	Sugars	3g
Protein	29g	Fat	47g
Carbohydrate	32g	Saturates	15g

35 mins — 1 hr 10 mins

SERVES 6–8

INGREDIENTS

- 115 g/4 oz butter, plus extra 2 tbsp melted
- 2 onions, chopped finely
- 115 g/4 oz long-grain white rice
- 750 g/1 lb 10 oz skinned salmon fillet, poached in water, cooking liquid reserved
- 150 g/5½ oz mushrooms, thinly sliced
- 85 g/3 oz cooked spinach, chopped
- 2 tbsp chopped fresh dill
- 6 canned anchovy fillets in oil, drained and chopped
- 5 hard-boiled eggs, roughly chopped
- grated rind and juice of 1 large lemon
- 375 g/13 oz packet puff pastry
- 1 egg, beaten, for glaze
- salt and pepper

TO GARNISH

- lemon wedges
- dill sprigs

1 Melt half of the butter in a large saucepan, add half the onion and cook for about 2 minutes, or until soft. Stir in the rice for 2 minutes, or until well coated.

2 Add water to make the reserved fish cooking liquid up to 225 ml/8 fl oz. Add to the rice, bring to the boil, cover and cook gently for 18 minutes, then let cool.

3 Melt the remaining butter in a frying pan, add the remaining onions and the sliced mushrooms and cook for about 8 minutes, or until the liquid has been absorbed. Add the cooked spinach and fresh dill. Season well, then cool.

4 Add the anchovies, eggs and lemon rind and juice to the mushroom mixture and toss well.

5 Roll out the puff pastry and cut into two squares, one 28 cm/11 inches across and the other 30 cm/12 inches across. Place the smaller pastry square on a lightly greased baking tray and spread half the mushroom mixture over, leaving a 2.5 cm/1 inch border around the edge. Spoon over half the rice.

6 Centre the salmon on top of the rice layer and cover with the remaining rice. Spoon over the remaining mushroom mixture. Drizzle the melted butter over the top. Brush the pastry edges with egg, cover with the larger square and seal the edges.

7 Brush with egg and bake in a preheated oven, 220°C/425°F/Gas Mark 7, for about 35 minutes, or until golden. Rest on a wire rack, then serve garnished with lemon wedges and dill sprigs.

5

6

Fried Rice with Prawns

Strong seafood flavours complement plain rice in this satisfying dish, which works equally well with large peeled prawns or tiger prawns.

NUTRITIONAL INFORMATION

Calories	599	Sugars	0g
Protein	26g	Fat	16g
Carbohydrate	94g	Saturates	3g

5 mins — 35 mins

SERVES 4

INGREDIENTS

- 300 g/10½ oz long-grain rice
- 2 eggs
- 4 tsp cold water
- 3 tbsp sunflower oil
- 4 spring onions, thinly sliced diagonally
- 1 garlic clove, crushed
- 125 g/4½ oz closed-cup or button mushrooms, sliced thinly
- 2 tbsp oyster or anchovy sauce
- 200 g/7 oz canned water chestnuts, drained and sliced
- 250 g/9 oz peeled prawns, defrosted if frozen
- salt and pepper
- chopped watercress, to garnish (optional)

1 Bring a saucepan of lightly salted water to the boil. Sprinkle in the rice, return to the boil, then reduce the heat and simmer for 15–20 minutes, or until tender. Drain, rinse under hot running water, then drain again. Keep warm.

2 Beat each egg separately with 2 teaspoons of cold water and salt and pepper.

3 Heat 2 teaspoons of sunflower oil in a wok or large frying pan, swirling it around until really hot. Pour in the first egg, swirl it around and let cook undisturbed until set. Remove to a plate or board and repeat with the second egg. Cut the omelettes into 2.5 cm/1 inch squares.

4 Heat the remaining oil in the wok and when really hot add the spring onions and garlic and cook for 1 minute. Add the mushrooms and cook for a further 2 minutes.

5 Stir in the oyster or anchovy sauce and season with salt and pepper, add the water chestnuts and prawns, and stir-fry for 2 minutes.

6 Stir in the cooked rice and stir-fry for 1 minute, then add the omelette squares and stir-fry for a further 1-2 minutes until piping hot. Serve at once garnished with chopped watercress, if liked.

3

4

5

Crab Fried Rice

Canned crabmeat is used in this recipe for convenience, but fresh white crabmeat could be used – quite deliciously – in its place.

NUTRITIONAL INFORMATION

Calories	225	Sugars	1g
Protein	12g	Fat	11g
Carbohydrate	20g	Saturates	2g

5 mins 25 mins

SERVES 4

INGREDIENTS

- 150 g/5½ oz long-grain rice
- 2 tbsp groundnut oil
- 125 g/4½ oz canned white crabmeat, drained
- 1 leek, sliced
- 150 g/5½ oz beansprouts
- 2 eggs, beaten
- 1 tbsp light soy sauce
- 2 tsp lime juice
- 1 tsp sesame oil
- salt
- sliced lime, to garnish

1 Cook the rice in a saucepan of boiling salted water for 15 minutes. Drain well, rinse under cold running water and drain again thoroughly.

2 Heat the groundnut oil in a preheated wok until it is really hot.

3 Add the crabmeat, sliced leek and beansprouts to the wok and stir-fry for 2–3 minutes, then remove the mixture from the wok using a slotted spoon and set aside.

4 Add the eggs to the wok and cook, stirring occasionally, for 2–3 minutes, or until they begin to set.

5 Stir the rice and the crabmeat, leek and beansprout mixture into the eggs in the wok.

6 Add the soy sauce and lime juice to the mixture in the wok. Cook for 1 minute, stirring to combine, and sprinkle with the sesame oil.

7 Transfer the crab fried rice to a serving dish, garnish with the sliced lime and serve immediately.

3

5

6

VARIATION

Cooked lobster may be used instead of the crab for a really special dish.

Lemon & Basil Rice

Jasmine rice has a delicate flavour and can be served plain. In this dish, the light tang of lemon and soft scent of basil add an extra touch.

NUTRITIONAL INFORMATION			
Calories	384	Sugars	0g
Protein	7g	Fat	4g
Carbohydrate	86g	Saturates	1g

15 mins   15 mins

SERVES 4

INGREDIENTS

- 400 g/14 oz jasmine rice
- 800 ml/1⅓ pints water
- finely grated rind of ½ lemon
- 2 tbsp chopped fresh sweet basil

1 Wash the rice in several changes of cold water until the water runs clear. Bring a large pan of water to the boil, then add the rice.

2 Bring back to a rolling boil. Turn the heat to a low simmer, cover the pan and simmer for a further 12 minutes.

3 Remove the pan from the heat and let stand, covered, for 10 minutes.

4 Fluff up the rice with a fork, then stir in the lemon. Serve scattered with chopped fresh basil.

1

2

4

COOK'S TIP

It is important to leave the pan tightly covered while the rice cooks and steams inside so the grains cook evenly and become fluffy and separate.

Rice Noodles with Spinach

This dish makes a delicious light lunch in minutes. You can leave out the prawns, or replace them with chopped peanuts for a vegetarian dish.

NUTRITIONAL INFORMATION

Calories	159	Sugars	3g
Protein	8g	Fat	2g
Carbohydrate	27g	Saturates	0.1g

35 mins   5 mins

SERVES 4

INGREDIENTS

- 115 g/4 oz thin rice stick noodles
- 2 tbsp dried prawns (optional)
- 250 g/9 oz fresh young spinach
- 1 tbsp groundnut oil
- 2 garlic cloves, chopped finely
- 2 tsp Thai green curry paste
- 1 tsp sugar
- 1 tbsp light soy sauce

1 Soak the noodles in hot water for 15 minutes, or according to the packet instructions, then drain well.

2 Soak the prawns in hot water for 10 minutes and drain. Wash the spinach, thoroughly, drain well, and remove any tough stalks.

3 Heat the oil in a large frying pan or wok and stir-fry the garlic for 1 minute. Stir in the curry paste and stir-fry for 30 seconds. Stir in the soaked shrimp and stir-fry for 30 seconds.

4 Add the spinach and stir-fry for 1-2 minutes until the leaves are just wilted.

5 Stir in the sugar and soy sauce, then add the noodles and toss thoroughly to mix evenly. Serve immediately while hot.

COOK'S TIP

Young, tender spinach leaves which cook in seconds are best for this dish. If you use older spinach shred the leaves before adding to the dish, so they cook more quickly.

Rice with Black Beans

Any kind of bean cooking liquid is delicious for cooking rice – black beans are particularly good for their startling grey colour and earthy flavour.

NUTRITIONAL INFORMATION

Calories	252	Sugars	2g
Protein	5g	Fat	8g
Carbohydrate	43g	Saturates	1g

10 mins | 15 mins

SERVES 4

INGREDIENTS

- 1 onion, chopped
- 5 garlic cloves, chopped
- 225 ml/8 fl oz chicken or vegetable stock
- 2 tbsp vegetable oil
- 175 g/6 oz long-grain rice
- 225 ml/8 fl oz liquid from cooking black beans (including some black beans)
- ½ tsp ground cumin
- salt and pepper

TO GARNISH

- 3–5 spring onions, thinly sliced
- 2 tbsp chopped fresh coriander leaves

1. Put the onion in a blender with the garlic and stock and blend until the consistency of a chunky sauce.

2. Heat the oil in a heavy-based pan and cook the rice until it is golden. Add the onion mixture, with the cooking liquid from the black beans (and any beans). Add the cumin, with salt and pepper to taste.

3. Cover the pan and cook over a medium-low heat for about 10 minutes until the rice is tender and coloured evenly by the black bean liquid.

4. Fluff up the rice with a fork, and let rest for about 5 minutes, covered. Serve sprinkled with thinly sliced spring onions and chopped coriander.

2

3

4

VARIATION

Instead of black beans, use pinto beans or chickpeas. Proceed as above and serve with any savoury spicy sauce, or as an accompaniment to roasted meat.

Mango & Wild Rice Salad

Wild rice is, in fact, an aquatic grass that is native to North America. It has a delicious nutty flavour and a slightly chewy texture.

NUTRITIONAL INFORMATION			
Calories	320	Sugars	10g
Protein	6g	Fat	20g
Carbohydrate	30g	Saturates	2g

15 mins   45–50 mins

SERVES 4

INGREDIENTS

- 75 g/2¾ oz wild rice
- 150 g/5½ oz Basmati rice
- 3 tbsp hazelnut oil
- 1 tbsp sherry vinegar
- 1 ripe mango
- 3 celery sticks
- 75 g/2¾ oz ready-to-eat dried apricots, chopped
- 75 g/2¾ oz flaked almonds, toasted
- 2 tbsp chopped fresh coriander or mint
- salt and pepper
- sprigs of fresh coriander or mint, to garnish

1

4

5

1 Cook the rice in separate saucepans in lightly salted boiling water. Cook the wild rice for 45–50 minutes and the basmati rice for 10–12 minutes. Drain, rinse well and drain again. Place the rice in a large bowl and let cool.

2 Mix the oil, vinegar and seasoning. Pour over the rice and toss well.

3 Cut the mango in half lengthways, as close to the stone as possible. Remove and discard the stone.

4 Peel the skin from the mango and cut the flesh into slices.

5 Slice the celery thinly and add to the cooled rice with the mango, apricots, almonds and chopped herbs. Toss together and transfer to a serving dish.

6 Garnish the salad with sprigs of fresh coriander or mint.

COOK'S TIP

To toast almonds, place them on a baking tray in a preheated oven, 180°C/350°F/Gas Mark 4, for 5–10 minutes., or toast them under the grill, turning them frequently and checking frequently that they do not burn.

Greek-style Rice Salad

An ideal accompaniment to barbecued lamb or chicken, with all the flavours of the Aegean – lemon, feta cheese, capers, tomatoes and olives.

NUTRITIONAL INFORMATION			
Calories	365	Sugars	4g
Protein	9g	Fat	23g
Carbohydrate	31g	Saturates	7g

5 mins 15–20 mins

SERVES 4–6

INGREDIENTS

- 200 g/7 oz long-grain white rice
- 85 ml/3 fl oz extra virgin olive oil
- 2–3 tbsp lemon juice
- 1 tbsp chopped fresh oregano or 1 tsp dried oregano
- ½ tsp Dijon mustard
- 2 large ripe tomatoes, deseeded and chopped
- 1 red or green pepper, deseeded and chopped
- 75 g/2¾ oz Kalamata or other brine-cured black olives, stoned and halved
- 225 g/8 oz feta cheese, crumbled, plus extra cubes, to garnish
- 1 tbsp capers, rinsed and drained
- 2–4 tbsp chopped fresh flat-leaved parsley or coriander
- salt and pepper
- diced cucumber, to garnish

1 Bring a saucepan of water to the boil. Add a teaspoon of salt, sprinkle in the rice and return to the boil, stirring once or twice. Reduce the heat and simmer for 15–20 minutes, or until the rice is tender, stirring once or twice. Drain, rinse under hot running water and drain again.

2 Meanwhile, whisk together the olive oil, lemon juice, oregano, mustard and salt and pepper in a bowl. Add the tomatoes, pepper, olives, feta cheese, capers and parsley and stir to coat in the dressing. Let marinate for 10 minute.

3 Turn the rice into a large bowl with the marinated vegetable mixture, and toss to mix well.

4 Season the salad with salt and pepper to taste, then divide between 4–6 individual dishes and garnish with extra feta cheese cubes and diced cucumber. Serve just warm.

2

3

4

VARIATION

This salad is also delicious made with brown rice – just increase the cooking time to 25–30 minutes.

Wild Rice & Scallop Salad

Wild rice has a nutty texture, which is great in salads. The smokiness of the bacon and the sweetness of the scallops make a perfect combination.

NUTRITIONAL INFORMATION

Calories	580	Sugars	1g
Protein	19g	Fat	41g
Carbohydrate	35g	Saturates	6g

5 mins · 35–55 mins

SERVES 4

INGREDIENTS

150 g/5½ oz wild rice

600 ml/1 pint water, or more if necessary

50 g/1¾ oz pecan nuts or walnuts

2 tbsp vegetable oil

4 slices smoked bacon, diced or sliced

3–4 shallots, chopped finely

80 ml/3 fl oz walnut oil

2–3 tbsp sherry or cider vinegar

2 tbsp chopped fresh dill

8–12 large scallops, cut lengthways in half

salt and pepper

lemon and lime slices, to serve

4

5

6

1 Put the wild rice in a saucepan with the water and bring to the boil, stirring once or twice. Reduce the heat to low, cover, and simmer gently for 30–50 minutes, depending on whether you prefer a chewy or tender texture. Using a fork, fluff the rice into a large bowl, then let cool slightly.

2 Meanwhile, toast the nuts in a frying pan for 2–3 minutes, or until just beginning to colour, stirring frequently. Cool, chop roughly, and set aside.

3 Heat a tablespoon of the vegetable oil in the pan. Stir in the bacon and cook, stirring occasionally, until crisp and brown. Transfer to kitchen paper to drain. Remove some of the oil from the pan and stir in the shallots. Cook for 3–4 minutes, stirring from time to time, until soft.

4 Stir the toasted nuts, bacon and shallots into the rice. Add the walnut oil, vinegar, half the chopped dill and salt and pepper to taste. Toss well to combine the ingredients, then set aside.

5 Brush a large non-stick frying pan with the remaining oil. Heat until very hot, add the scallops and cook for 1 minute on each side until golden. Do not overcook.

6 Divide the wild rice salad among individual serving plates. Top with the scallops and sprinkle with the remaining dill. Garnish with a sprig of dill, if desired and serve immediately with the lemon and lime slices.

Gazpacho Rice Salad

This rice dish has all the flavours of a zesty Spanish gazpacho. Garlic, tomatoes, peppers, cucumber and rice make it a great summer salad.

NUTRITIONAL INFORMATION

Calories	253	Sugars	15g
Protein	7g	Fat	5g
Carbohydrate	46g	Saturates	1g

35–40 mins 30 mins

SERVES 4–6

INGREDIENTS

- extra virgin olive oil
- 1 onion, chopped finely
- 4 garlic cloves, chopped finely
- 200 g/7 oz long-grain white rice or basmati
- 350 ml/12 fl oz vegetable stock or water
- 1½ tsp dried thyme
- 3 tbsp sherry vinegar
- 1 tsp Dijon mustard
- 1 tsp honey or sugar
- 1 red pepper, cored, deseeded and chopped
- ½ yellow pepper, cored, deseeded and chopped
- ½ green pepper, cored, deseeded and chopped
- 1 red onion, finely chopped
- ½ cucumber, peeled, deseeded and chopped (optional)
- 3 tomatoes, deseeded and chopped
- 2–3 tbsp chopped flat-leaved parsley
- salt and pepper

TO SERVE

- 12 cherry tomatoes, halved
- 12 black olives, stoned and roughly chopped
- 1 tbsp flaked almonds, toasted

1 Heat 2 tablespoons of the oil in a large saucepan. Add the onion and cook for 2 minutes, stirring frequently, or until beginning to soften. Stir in half the garlic and cook for a further minute.

2 Add the rice, stirring well to coat, and cook for about 2 minutes, or until translucent. Stir in the stock and half the thyme, bring to the boil, and season with salt and pepper. Simmer very gently, covered, for about 20 minutes, until tender. Stand, still covered, for about 15 minutes, then uncover and cool a little more.

3 Whisk the vinegar with the remaining garlic and thyme, and the mustard, honey and salt and pepper in a large bowl. Slowly whisk in about 80 ml/3 fl oz of the olive oil. Using a fork, fluff the rice into the vinaigrette.

4 Add the peppers, red onion, cucumber, tomatoes and parsley. Toss and season.

5 Transfer to a serving bowl and garnish with the tomatoes, olives and almonds. Serve warm.

3

4

5

Rice, Lentil & Shiitake Salad

Fresh shiitakes, a Japanese ingredient now more widely available, give this substantial salad a rich mushroomy flavour.

NUTRITIONAL INFORMATION

Calories	469	Sugars	24g
Protein	11g	Fat	22g
Carbohydrate	60g	Saturates	3g

5 mins 1½ hrs

SERVES 6–8

INGREDIENTS

- 225 g/8 oz Puy lentils, rinsed
- 4 tbsp olive oil
- 1 onion, chopped finely
- 200 g/7 oz long-grain brown rice
- ½ tsp dried thyme
- 450 ml/16 fl oz chicken stock
- 350 g/12 oz shiitake mushrooms, trimmed and sliced
- 2 garlic cloves, chopped finely
- 115 g/4 oz smoked bacon, diced and fried until crisp
- 2 small courgettes, diced
- 1–2 celery sticks, thinly sliced
- 6 spring onions, thinly sliced
- 2–3 tbsp chopped fresh flat-leaved parsley
- 2 tbsp walnut halves, toasted and roughly chopped
- salt and pepper

DRESSING

- 2 tbsp red or white wine vinegar
- 1 tbsp balsamic vinegar
- 1 tsp Dijon mustard
- 1 tsp sugar
- 80 ml/3 fl oz extra virgin olive oil
- 2–3 tbsp walnut oil

1

3

5

1 Bring a large saucepan of water to the boil. Add the lentils, bring back to the boil, then simmer for about 30 minutes, or until just tender – do not overcook. Drain, rinse under cold running water, drain again and set aside.

2 Heat 2 tablespoons of the olive oil in a large saucepan. Add the onion and cook until it begins to soften. Add the rice and stir, until well coated in the oil. Add the thyme, chicken stock and salt and pepper, and bring the mixture to the boil. Simmer very gently, covered tightly, for about 40 minutes, or until the rice is tender and the liquid absorbed.

3 Heat the remaining oil in a frying pan and stir-fry the mushrooms for about 5 minutes, or until golden. Stir in the garlic and cook for a further 30 seconds. Season with salt and pepper.

4 To make the dressing, whisk together the vinegars, mustard and sugar in a large bowl. Gradually whisk in the oils. Season with salt and pepper. Add the lentils and gently toss. Fork in the rice and toss.

5 Stir in the bacon and mushrooms, the courgettes, celery, spring onions and parsley. Season the salad to taste and serve sprinkled with walnuts.

Pesto Risotto-rice Salad

This is half risotto and half rice salad. Risotto rice produces quite a heavy salad, but substituting long-grain white rice makes a lighter version.

NUTRITIONAL INFORMATION

Calories	406	Sugars	5g
Protein	7g	Fat	28g
Carbohydrate	34g	Saturates	5g

40 mins | 30 mins

SERVES 4–6

INGREDIENTS

extra virgin olive oil
1 onion, chopped finely
200 g/7 oz arborio rice
450 ml/16 fl oz boiling water
6 sun-dried tomatoes, cut into thin slivers
½ small red onion, sliced very thinly
3 tbsp lemon juice

PESTO
55 g/2 oz lightly packed fresh basil leaves
2 garlic cloves, chopped finely
2 tbsp pine kernels, lightly toasted
125 ml/4 fl oz extra virgin olive oil
50 g/1¾ oz freshly grated Parmesan cheese
salt and pepper

TO GARNISH
fresh basil leaves
Parmesan cheese shavings

1 For the pesto, put the basil, garlic and pine kernels in a food processor and process for 30 seconds. With the machine running, gradually pour in the olive oil through the feed tube, until a smooth paste forms. Switch off, add the cheese, then pulse several times, until blended but still with some texture. Scrape the pesto into a small bowl, season with salt and pepper to taste, and set aside for later use.

2 Heat 1 tablespoon of the oil in a saucepan. Add the onion and cook until it begins to soften. Add the rice and stir to coat. Cook, stirring occasionally, for about 2 minutes. Stir in the boiling water, salt and pepper. Cover and simmer gently for 20 minutes, until the rice is just tender and the water absorbed. Cool slightly.

3 Put the sun-dried tomatoes and sliced onion in a large bowl, add the lemon juice and about 2 tablespoons of oil. Fork in the hot rice and stir in the pesto. Toss to combine. Adjust the seasoning if necessary. Cover and cool to room temperature.

4 Fork the rice mixture into a shallow serving bowl. Drizzle with some olive oil and garnish with basil leaves and Parmesan shavings. Serve the salad at room temperature, not chilled.

1

3

3
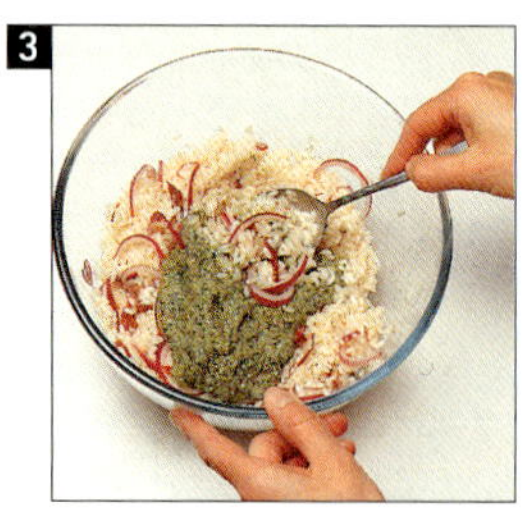

Thai Noodles with Prawns

This delicious mix of rice noodles and prawns, lightly dressed with typical Thai flavours, makes an impressive first course or a light lunch.

NUTRITIONAL INFORMATION

Calories	204	Sugars	8g
Protein	15g	Fat	3g
Carbohydrate	29g	Saturates	1g

10 mins 3 mins

SERVES 4

INGREDIENTS

- 85 g/3 oz rice vermicelli or rice sticks
- 175 g/6 oz mangetout, cut crossways in half if large
- 5 tbsp lime juice
- 4 tbsp Thai fish sauce
- 1 tbsp sugar, or to taste
- 2 tsp finely chopped fresh root ginger
- 1 red chilli, deseeded and sliced thinly on the diagonal
- 4 tbsp chopped fresh coriander or mint, plus extra for garnishing
- 10 cm/4 inch piece of cucumber, peeled, deseeded and diced
- 2 spring onions, sliced thinly on the diagonal
- 16–20 large cooked, peeled prawns
- 2 tbsp chopped unsalted peanuts or cashews (optional)
- 4 whole cooked prawns and lemon slices, to garnish

1 Put the rice noodles in a large bowl and pour over enough hot water to cover. Stand for about 4 minutes, or until soft. Drain, rinse under cold running water, drain again, then set aside.

2 Bring a saucepan of water to the boil. Add the mangetout and return to the boil. Simmer for 1 minute. Drain, rinse under cold running water until cold, then drain and set aside.

3 In a large bowl, whisk together the lime juice, fish sauce, sugar, ginger, chilli and coriander. Stir in the cucumber and spring onions. Add the drained noodles, mangetout and prawns and toss gently.

4 Divide the noodle salad among large serving plates. Sprinkle with chopped coriander and the peanuts (if using), then garnish each plate with a whole prawn and a lemon slice. Serve immediately.

3

3

4

COOK'S TIP

Rice noodles come in many sizes. For this light salad use the very thin variety, called rice vermicelli, rice sticks, or sen mee.

Coconut-scented Rice

This tender, creamy, aromatic rice makes an excellent accompaniment to grilled chicken, pork or fish.

NUTRITIONAL INFORMATION	
Calories 127	Sugars 2g
Protein 2g	Fat 1g
Carbohydrate . . 29g	Saturates 0.1g

5 mins | 50 mins

SERVES 4–6

INGREDIENTS

- 350 ml/12 fl oz water
- 225 ml/8 fl oz coconut milk
- 1 tsp salt
- 200 g/7 oz long-grain brown rice
- 1 lemon
- 1 cinnamon stick
- about 15 whole cloves
- 1 tbsp chopped fresh parsley
- fresh coconut shavings (optional)

1 Bring the water to the boil in a heavy-based saucepan and whisk in the coconut milk. Return the liquid to the boil, add the salt and sprinkle in the rice.

2 Pare 2–3 strips of lemon rind and add to the saucepan with the cinnamon stick and the cloves.

3 Reduce the heat to low, cover and simmer gently for about 45 minutes, or until the rice is tender and the liquid is completely absorbed. Uncover and turn the heat up to high for about 1 minute, to let any steam escape and make sure the rice dries out a little.

4 Remove the cloves, if wished, then sprinkle with the parsley and coconut shavings, if using. Fork into a warmed serving bowl and serve.

COOK'S TIP

This technique can be used to cook white rice, but the fuller flavour of brown rice works well with the warm flavours of the spices in this dish.

1

2

4

Thai Rice Pudding

This mildly spiced, creamy pudding with a rich custard topping is excellent served warm, and even better served cold the next day.

NUTRITIONAL INFORMATION

Calories	351	Sugars	16g
Protein	7g	Fat	21g
Carbohydrate	37g	Saturates	16g

10–15 mins   1–1¼ hrs

SERVES 4

INGREDIENTS

- 100 g/3½ oz short-grain rice
- 2 tbsp palm sugar
- 1 cardamom pod, split
- 300 ml/10 fl oz coconut milk
- 150 ml/5 fl oz water
- 3 eggs
- 200 ml/7 fl oz coconut cream
- 1 tbsp caster sugar
- fresh fruit, to serve
- sweetened coconut flakes, to decorate

2

3

4

1 Place the rice and palm sugar in a pan. Crush the seeds from the cardamom pod in a pestle and mortar and add to the pan. Stir in the coconut milk and water.

2 Bring to the boil, stirring, to dissolve the sugar. Lower the heat and simmer, uncovered, stirring occasionally for about 20 minutes until the rice is tender and most of the liquid is absorbed.

3 Spoon the cooked rice into ovenproof dishes and spread evenly. Place the dishes in a wide roasting tin, and fill it with water to reach halfway up their sides.

4 Beat together the eggs, coconut cream and caster sugar and spoon over the rice. Cover with foil and bake in a preheated oven, 180°C/350°F/Gas Mark 4, for 45–50 minutes, until the custard sets.

5 Serve warm or cold with fresh fruit, decorated with coconut flakes.

COOK'S TIP

Cardamom is quite a powerful spice. If you find it too strong it can be left out altogether, or replaced with a little ground cinnamon.

Lemon & Pistachio Pudding

This creamy, family-style dessert is ideal served well chilled at the height of summer with a mixture of seasonal berries.

NUTRITIONAL INFORMATION

Calories	332	Sugars	22g
Protein	11g	Fat	10g
Carbohydrate	52g	Saturates	3g

1¾ hrs — 25 mins

SERVES 4

INGREDIENTS

- 1 tsp cornflour
- 850 ml/1½ pints milk, plus an extra 2 tbsp
- 125 g/4½ oz short-grain rice
- about 2 tbsp sugar, or 1 tbsp honey, to taste
- finely grated rind of 1 large lemon
- freshly squeezed lemon juice, to taste
- 50 g/1¾ oz shelled pistachio nuts

1 Place the cornflour in a small bowl and stir in 2 tablespoons of milk, stirring until there are no lumps. Rinse a pan with cold water and do not dry it out.

2 Place the remaining milk and the cornflour mixture in the pan over a medium-high heat, stirring occasionally, until it simmers and forms small bubbles around the edge. Do not boil.

3 Stir in the rice, lower the heat and continue stirring for 20 minutes, or until all but about 2 tablespoons of the excess liquid has evaporated and the rice grains are tender.

4 Remove from the heat and pour into a heatproof bowl. Stir in sugar to taste, and the lemon rind. If a slightly tarter flavour is required, stir in freshly squeezed lemon juice. Let cool completely.

5 Tightly cover the top of the cooled rice with a sheet of cling film and chill in the refrigerator for at least 1 hour – the colder the rice is, the better it tastes with fresh fruit.

6 Meanwhile, using a sharp knife, finely chop the pistachio nuts. To serve, spoon the rice pudding into individual serving bowls and sprinkle with the chopped nuts.

COOK'S TIP

It is important to rinse the saucepan in step 1 to prevent the milk scorching on the sides or base of the pan.

3

4

6

Florentine Rice Pudding

This very sophisticated rice pudding from Florence is like a cross between a mousse and a soufflé, and is best served warm.

NUTRITIONAL INFORMATION

Calories	836	Sugars	127g
Protein	14g	Fat	25g
Carbohydrate	148g	Saturates	14g

20 mins | 50–55 mins

SERVES 6

INGREDIENTS

- 150 g/5½ oz long-grain white rice or Italian arborio rice
- pinch of salt
- 1 litre/1¾ pints milk
- 5 eggs
- 400 g/14 oz sugar or 450 g/1 lb honey, or a mixture
- 115 g/4 oz butter, melted and cooled
- 2 tbsp orange flower water or 4 tbsp orange-flavoured liqueur
- 225 g/8 oz diced candied orange peel
- 225 g/8 oz orange marmalade
- 2–3 tablespoons water
- icing sugar, for dusting

2

3

3

1 Put the rice and salt in a large heavy-bottomed saucepan. Add the milk and bring to the boil, stirring occasionally. Reduce the heat to low and simmer gently for about 25 minutes, or until the rice is tender and creamy. Remove from the heat.

2 Pass the cooked rice through a food mill into a large bowl. Alternatively, process in a food processor for about 30 seconds until smooth, then place in a bowl. Set aside, stirring from time to time to prevent a skin forming.

3 Meanwhile, using an electric mixer, beat the eggs with the sugar in a large bowl for about 4 minutes, or until very light and creamy. Gently fold into the rice with the melted butter. Stir in half of the orange flower water, then stir in the candied orange peel.

4 Turn the mixture into a well-buttered 2 litre/3½ pint soufflé dish. Place the dish in a roasting tin and pour in enough boiling water to come 4 cm/1½ inches up the side of the dish.

5 Bake in a preheated oven, 180°C/350°F/Gas Mark 4, for about 25 minutes, or until puffed and lightly set. Transfer the dish to a wire rack to cool slightly.

6 Heat the marmalade with the water, stirring until it is dissolved and completely smooth. Stir in the remaining orange flower water and pour the mixture into a sauceboat. Dust the top of the rice pudding with the icing sugar and serve warm with the marmalade sauce.

Chocolate Rice Dessert

What could be more delicious than creamy tender rice cooked in a rich chocolate sauce? This dessert is almost like a dense chocolate mousse.

NUTRITIONAL INFORMATION

Calories	336	Sugars	26g
Protein	4g	Fat	20g
Carbohydrate	35g	Saturates	13g

2½ hrs | 1 hr 10 mins

SERVES 8

INGREDIENTS

- 100 g/3½ oz long-grain white rice
- pinch of salt
- 600 ml/1 pint milk
- 100 g/3½ oz granulated sugar
- 200 g/7 oz bitter or dark chocolate, chopped
- 5 tbsp butter, diced
- 1 tsp vanilla essence
- 2 tbsp brandy or Cognac
- 175 ml/6 fl oz double cream
- whipped cream, for piping (optional)
- chocolate curls, to decorate (optional)

1 Bring a saucepan of water to the boil. Sprinkle in the rice and add the salt, then reduce the heat and simmer gently for 15–20 minutes, or until the rice is just tender. Drain, rinse, and drain again.

2 Heat the milk and the sugar in a large heavy-based saucepan over a medium heat until the sugar dissolves, stirring frequently. Add the chocolate and butter and stir until melted and smooth.

3 Stir in the cooked rice and reduce the heat to low. Cover and simmer, stirring occasionally, for 30 minutes, or until the milk is absorbed and the mixture thickened. Stir in the vanilla essence and brandy. Remove the mixture from the heat and let cool to room temperature.

4 Using an electric mixer, beat the cream until soft peaks form. Stir one heaped spoonful of the cream into the chocolate rice mixture to lighten it, then fold in the remaining cream.

5 Spoon into glass serving dishes, cover and chill for about 2 hours. If wished, decorate with piped whipped cream and top with chocolate curls. Serve cold.

VARIATION

To mould the chocolate rice, soften 1 sachet of gelatine in about 50 ml/2 fl oz of cold water and heat gently until dissolved. Stir into the chocolate just before folding in the cream. Pour into a rinsed mould, allow to set, then unmould.

Orange-scented Rice

This delicious creamy pudding is flavoured with ginger, fresh oranges and orange-flavoured liqueur for a wonderfully aromatic result.

NUTRITIONAL INFORMATION

Calories	412	Sugars	64g
Protein	7g	Fat	6g
Carbohydrate	82g	Saturates	4g

30 mins 50 mins

SERVES 6

INGREDIENTS

- 140 g/5 oz pudding rice
- 225 ml/8 fl oz freshly squeezed orange juice
- pinch of salt
- 500 ml/18 fl oz milk
- 1 vanilla pod, split
- 5 cm/2 inch piece fresh root ginger, peeled and gently bruised
- 200 g/7 oz sugar
- 50 ml/2 fl oz double cream
- 4 tbsp orange-flavoured liqueur
- 2 tbsp butter
- 4–6 seedless oranges
- 2 pieces stem ginger, sliced thinly, plus 2 tbsp ginger syrup from the jar
- ground ginger, for dusting

2

4

5

1 Put the rice in a large heavy-based saucepan with the orange juice and salt. Bring to the boil, skimming off any foam. Reduce the heat to low and simmer gently for about 10 minutes, stirring occasionally, until the juice is absorbed.

2 Gradually stir in the milk, add the vanilla pod and ginger root and continue simmering for 30 minutes, stirring frequently, until the milk is absorbed and the rice is tender. Remove from the heat and remove the vanilla pod and ginger root.

3 Stir in half the sugar, half the cream, the orange liqueur and the butter until the sugar is dissolved and the butter is melted. Let cool, stir in the remaining cream and pour into a serving bowl. Leave, covered, at room temperature.

4 Pare the rind from the oranges and reserve. Working over a bowl to catch the juices, remove the pith from all the oranges. Cut out the segments and drop into the bowl. Stir in the stem ginger and syrup. Chill in the refrigerator.

5 Meanwhile, cut the pared orange rind into very thin strips and blanch for 1 minute. Drain and rinse. Bring 225 ml/8 fl oz of water to the boil with the remaining sugar. Add the rind strips and simmer gently until the syrup is reduced by half, then let cool.

6 Serve the pudding in a decorative dish or in individual glass cups. Decorate with the chilled oranges, then top the pudding with the caramelized orange rind strips and dust it with ginger.

Lebanese Almond Rice

This rice cream is flavoured with almonds and rosewater. If pomegranates are in season, decorate with the fruit's pink seeds for a stunning effect.

NUTRITIONAL INFORMATION

Calories	199	Sugars	17g
Protein	7g	Fat	9g
Carbohydrate	23g	Saturates	2g

15 mins 2¾ hrs

SERVES 6

INGREDIENTS

- 5 tbsp rice flour
- pinch of salt
- 700 ml/1¼ pints milk
- 5 tbsp caster sugar
- 85 g/3 oz ground almonds
- 1 tbsp rosewater

TO DECORATE

- 2 tbsp chopped pistachio nuts or toasted flaked almonds
- pomegranate seeds (optional)
- washed rose petals (optional)

1 Put the rice flour in a bowl, stir in the salt and make a well in the centre. Pour in about 50 ml/2 fl oz of the milk and whisk to form a smooth paste.

2 Bring the remaining milk to the boil in a heavy-based saucepan. Whisk in the rice flour paste and the sugar and cook, stirring continuously, until the mixture thickens and bubbles. Reduce the heat and simmer gently for 5 minutes.

3 Whisk in the ground almonds until the pudding is smooth and thickened, then remove from the heat to cool slightly. Stir in the rosewater and cool completely, stirring occasionally.

4 Divide the mixture between 6 glasses or pour into a serving bowl. Chill for at least 2 hours before serving.

5 To serve, sprinkle with the chopped pistachios or toasted almonds, and with pomegranate seeds, if available. Scatter with rose petals, if wished.

1

2

3

COOK'S TIP

For a smoother texture, this can be made without the ground almonds. Stir 2 tablespoons of cornflour into the ground rice and use a little more of the milk to make the paste. Proceed as directed, omitting the ground almonds.

Portuguese Rice Pudding

This buttery, egg-rich rice pudding is quite irresistible, and makes a deliciously different dessert for a dinner party.

NUTRITIONAL INFORMATION

Calories	363	Sugars	22g
Protein	7g	Fat	19g
Carbohydrate	44g	Saturates	10g

10 mins — 35 mins

SERVES 6–8

INGREDIENTS

- 200 g/7 oz Spanish Valencia, Italian arborio or pudding rice
- pinch of salt
- 1 lemon
- 450 ml/16 fl oz milk
- 150 ml/5 fl oz single cream
- 1 cinnamon stick
- 6 tbsp butter
- 140 g/5 oz sugar (or to taste)
- 8 egg yolks
- ground cinnamon, for dusting
- thick or double cream, to serve

1 Bring a saucepan of water to the boil. Sprinkle in the rice and salt and return to the boil, then reduce the heat and simmer until just tender. Drain, rinse and drain again.

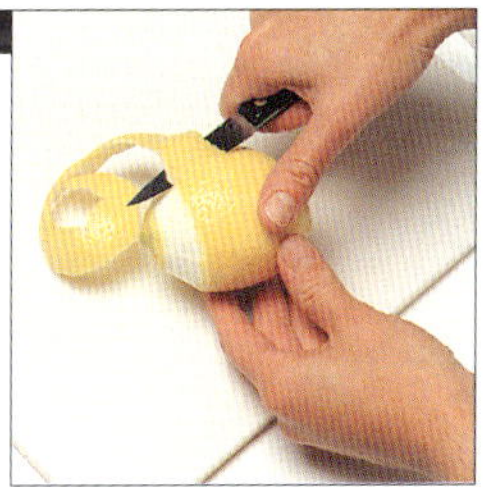

2

2 Using a small sharp knife or swivel-bladed vegetable peeler, and working in a circular motion, try to peel the rind off the lemon in one curly piece; this makes it easier to remove later. Alternatively, peel off in strips.

3

3 Place the milk and cream in a pan and bring to a simmer over a medium heat. Add the rice, cinnamon stick, butter and the lemon rind 'curl' or strips. Reduce the heat to low and simmer the mixture very gently for about 20 minutes, or until it becomes thick and creamy in consistency. Remove from the heat, and remove and discard the cinnamon stick and lemon rind. Stir in the sugar until dissolved.

4

4 In a large bowl, beat the egg yolks until well blended. Gradually beat in the rice mixture until smooth. Stir frequently, to prevent the eggs from curdling, until slightly cooled, then pour into a bowl or 6–8 individual glasses. Dust with ground cinnamon and serve at room temperature.

Rice Muffins with Amaretto

Italian rice gives these delicate muffins an interesting texture. The amaretti biscuits complement the flavours and add a crunchy topping.

NUTRITIONAL INFORMATION

Calories	230	Sugars	10g
Protein	5g	Fat	14g
Carbohydrate	22g	Saturates	7g

15 mins 15 mins

MAKES 12 MUFFINS

INGREDIENTS

- 140 g/5 oz plain flour
- 1 tbsp baking powder
- ½ tsp bicarbonate of soda
- ½ tsp salt
- 1 egg
- 50 ml/2 fl oz honey
- 125 ml/4 fl oz milk
- 2 tbsp sunflower oil
- ½ tsp almond essence
- 55 g/2 oz cooked arborio rice
- 2–3 amaretti biscuits, roughly crushed

AMARETTO BUTTER

- 115 g/4 oz unsalted butter, at room temperature
- 1 tbsp honey
- 1–2 tbsp Amaretto liqueur
- 1–2 tbsp mascarpone cheese

1 Sift the plain flour, baking powder, bicarbonate of soda and salt into a large bowl and mix together well. Make a well in the centre.

2 In another bowl, beat the egg, honey, milk, oil and almond essence with an electric mixer for about 2 minutes, or until light and foamy. Gradually beat in the rice. Pour into the well and, using a fork, stir lightly until just combined. Do not over-beat: the mixture can be slightly lumpy.

3 Spoon the batter into a lightly greased 12 cup muffin tin or two 6 cup tins. Sprinkle each portion of batter with some of the amaretti crumbs and bake in a preheated oven, 200°C/400°F/Gas Mark 6, for about 15 minutes, or until risen and golden. The tops should spring back lightly when pressed.

4 Cool in the pans on a wire rack for about 1 minute. Carefully remove the muffins and cool slightly.

5 To make the Amaretto butter, put the butter and honey in a small bowl and beat until creamy. Add the Amaretto and mascarpone and beat together. Spoon into a small serving bowl and serve with the warm muffins.

2

3

5

COOK'S TIP

Use paper liners to line the muffin pan cups and avoid sticking.

Sweet Risotto Cake

Served with your favourite summer berries and a scented mascarpone cream, this baked sweet risotto makes an unusual dessert.

NUTRITIONAL INFORMATION

Calories	319	Sugars	30g
Protein	8g	Fat	9g
Carbohydrate	54g	Saturates	4g

20 mins 25–30 mins

SERVES 6–8

INGREDIENTS

- 90 g/3¼ oz arborio rice
- 350 ml/12 fl oz milk
- 3–4 tbsp sugar
- ½ tsp freshly grated nutmeg
- ½ tsp salt, plus a pinch for the almond mixture
- 190 g/6½ oz plain flour
- 1½ tsp baking powder
- 1 tsp bicarbonate of soda
- 1–2 tbsp caster sugar
- 1 egg
- 175 ml/6 fl oz milk
- 125 ml/4 fl oz soured cream or yogurt
- 1 tbsp butter, melted
- 2 tbsp honey
- ½ tsp almond essence
- 2 tbsp toasted flaked almonds
- 2 tbsp melted butter, for greasing
- icing sugar, for dusting (optional)

MUSCAT BERRIES

- 450 g/1 lb mixed summer berries, such as strawberries (halved), raspberries and blueberries
- 50 ml/2 fl oz Muscat wine
- 1–2 tbsp sugar

1. Put the rice, milk, sugar, nutmeg and ½ teaspoon of salt in a heavy-based pan. Bring to the boil, reduce the heat slightly and cook, stirring constantly, until the rice is tender and the milk almost absorbed, then let cool.

2. Combine the flour, baking powder, bicarbonate of soda, pinch of salt and the caster sugar. In a bowl, beat the egg, milk, soured cream, butter, honey and almond essence with an electric mixer until smooth. Gradually beat in the rice. Stir in the flour mixture and the almonds.

3. Gently spoon the rice and almond mixture into a 23–25 cm/9–10 inch well-greased cake tin with a removable bottom, smoothing the top evenly. Bake in a preheated oven, 160°C/325°F/Gas Mark 3, for about 20 minutes until golden. Cool in the tin on a wire rack.

4. While the cake is cooking, put the berries in a bowl and add the sugar and wine. To make the mascarpone cream, stir all the ingredients together and chill.

5. Remove the sides of the tin and slide the cake gently on to a serving plate. Dust the cake with icing sugar and serve warm with the Muscat berries and mascarpone cream (pipe the cream on top of the cake, if liked).

2

3

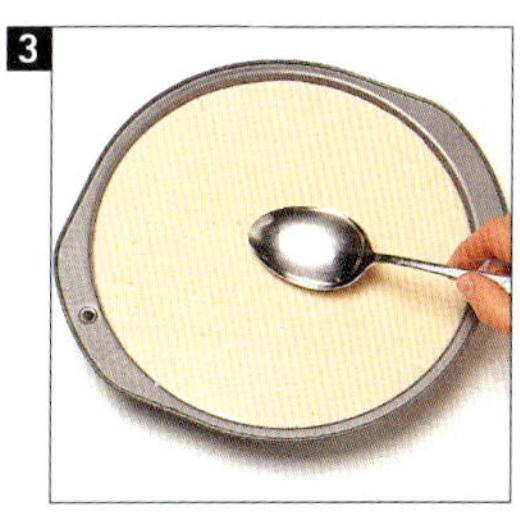

MASCARPONE CREAM

- 2 tbsp Muscat wine
- 1 tbsp honey
- ½ tsp almond essence
- 225 ml/8 fl oz mascarpone cheese

This is a Parragon Book
This edition published in 2002

Parragon
Queen Street House
4 Queen Street
Bath BA1 1HE, UK

ISBN: 0-75257-734-4

Printed in China

NOTE

This book uses metric and imperial measurements. Follow the same units of measurement throughout; do not mix metric and imperial. All spoon measurements are level: teaspoons are assumed to be 5 ml, and tablespoons are assumed to be 15 ml. Unless otherwise stated, milk is assumed to be full fat, eggs and individual vegetables such as potatoes are medium, and pepper is freshly ground black pepper.

The nutritional information provided for each recipe is per serving or per person. Optional ingredients, variations or serving suggestions have not been included in the calculations. The times given for each recipe are an approximate guide only because the preparation times may differ according to the techniques used by different people and the cooking times may vary as a result of the type of oven used.

Recipes using raw or very lightly cooked eggs should be avoided by infants, the elderly, pregnant women, convalescents, and anyone suffering from an illness.

The publisher would like to thank Steamer Trading Cookshop, Lewes, East Sussex, for the kind loan of props.